The Spiritual Way
of
St. Jeanne d'Arc

George H. Tavard

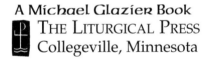

A Michael Glazier Book
THE LITURGICAL PRESS
Collegeville, Minnesota

A Michael Glazier Book published by The Liturgical Press

Cover design by David Manahan, O.S.B. Photo by Gene Plaisted, O.S.C. Joan of Arc, Cathedral of St-Etienne, Chalons-sur-Marne, France.

1	2	3	4	5	6	7	8

Library of Congress Cataloging-in-Publication Data

Tavard, George H. (George Henry), 1922–
    The spiritual way of St. Jeanne d'Arc / George H. Tavard.
      p. cm.
    "A Michael Glazier book."
    Includes index.
    ISBN 0-8146-5881-4 (alk. paper)
    1. Joan, of Arc, Saint, 1412–1431. 2. Christian saints—France—Biography. 3. Spirituality. 4. France—History—Charles VII, 1422–1461.
    I. Title.
DC103.T28   1998
944'.026'092—dc21
[B]   98-34305
                               CIP

Contents

Foreword

The present book was born in a meditation on Jeanne d'Arc that began in my childhood when I visited a number of times Domremy, Vaucouleurs, Toul, and other sites that were graced by her presence six centuries ago. Most of the many authors who have written on Jeanne have concentrated on the campaigns in which she took part, on her trial and condemnation by churchmen in Rouen, or on her so-called rehabilitation after her death. Many have discussed her voices and visions and suggested interpretations and explanations inspired by theories relating to history and the growth of nationalism, to psychology and the emergence of feminism, to comparative religion and perceived or imagined ties between folk religion, heterodoxy, sorcery, and witchcraft. Few have tried to analyze the structure and depth of her inner life. This is precisely what I have done. I have sought for the spiritual sources and resources of her rich personality.

In so doing it is necessary that I speak both of Jeanne's life and of her trial. Yet readers who are familiar with the details of the story may well skip the first chapter, devoted to the historical and political context in which she breathed. My study of Jeanne's spirituality discusses Jeanne's self-identity (ch. 2), her mission (ch. 3), the angels (ch. 4) and saints (ch. 5) whom she heard and saw, the night (ch. 6) and the fire (ch. 7) that she passed through, and finally the focus of all her thoughts and actions, which I find in the appellation, "daughter of God," by which her voices designated her (ch. 8). Because of the many problems raised by Jeanne's brief but intense passage in our world I have added five appendices, which could also be skipped by hurried readers.

It is impossible to study Jeanne d'Arc without being deeply indebted to the scholars who have made available the minutes of her trial and of the nullity investigation (often though inexactly called the "rehabilitation trial"): Jules Quicherat (abbreviated as Q in my notes) and, more recently, Pierre Tisset (abbreviated as T) and Pierre Duparc.

I gratefully dedicate this book to the memory of His Eminence Cardinal John J. Wright, former bishop of Worcester, Mass., and of Pittsburgh, Pa., a devotee of the girl from Domremy, who created a striking Joan of Arc chapel in the Catholic cathedral of Pittsburgh and who had the occasion to become for me a personal benefactor and friend.

George H. Tavard

ONE

The Historical and Political Context

Jeanne d'Arc and her career would not make sense outside her own time and place. She lived during the Hundred Years' War between the French and the English monarchies. She was born at the border between the kingdom of France and the duchy of Lorraine, which was itself part of the Holy Roman Empire of the German Nation.

It was a period of turmoil. The region where Jeanne lived as a child was never in the first line of battle. Yet the inhabitants were in constant fear lest roving bands of looters would come from the west, the north, or the southwest and burn what they could not steal. Only the east side was relatively secure. Between the village and the unmarked border of the duchy the castle of Bourlémont on an island in the river could offer temporary protection in time of danger. But the Lorraine town of Neufchâteau, eleven kilometers to the south, was still safer.

War in France

The kingdom of France was in deep trouble. What was later known as the Hundred Years' War—in reality a series of major battles, from Crécy (1346) and Azincourt (1415) to Verneuil (1424), Fermigny (1450), and Castillon (1453), separated by periods of skirmishes and truces[1]—had been occasioned

[1]The first three were English victories, the last two French victories. Although there can be no doubt that the turning point in the wars was due to Jeanne *la Pucelle* when she forced the English commanders to give up

1

by the claim of Edward III of England (1327–1377) in 1328 to be the rightful heir to the crown of France. His claim was founded on his lineage, for his mother, the wife of Edward II (1284–1327), was Isabelle, daughter of the king of France, Philippe IV *le Bel* (1268–1314). It was occasioned by the fact that at the death of Philippe V *le Long,* king of France, in 1328, the crown had been passed on by the Estates General of the kingdom to a nephew of Philippe *le Bel,* Philippe VI de Valois (1293–1350), rather than to his grandson, Edward III of England. This had been done by invoking the Salic law, a largely forgotten principle of the Salic Franks: women do not inherit the crown and cannot transmit it; it is transmitted only by and to men.

The claim of Edward III, however, was strengthened by the situation of Normandy. After the conquest of England in 1066 by William the Conqueror (1027–1087), duke of Normandy, the Saxon monarchs were replaced by the dukes of Normandy. Henceforth the kings of England were therefore dukes of Normandy. Though sovereign in England, they were vassals of the king of France for the territory of the duchy. They had a solid base from which to operate in France. And this base had been considerably widened when, in 1152, Aliénor d'Aquitaine (1122–1204), the repudiated wife of Louis VII of France, remarried Henry II Plantagenet (1154–1189), king of England, and brought him her lands of Aquitaine and Poitou.

The first major battles of the Hundred Years' War were disastrous for the French knights, largely because the English archers were armed with long bows that hit their target much farther and with greater power than the ordinary bows of the French archers. After the victory at Crécy (1346) the English soldiers had taken the city of Calais in 1347. After Azincourt (1415),[2] they entered Paris in 1419. In 1420 a deal was reached between the English commanders and the queen of France,

---

the siege of Orléans, her period of the Hundred Years' War was not marked by major battles but by the storming of a few cities and surrender of many others to Charles VII.

    [2]Usually called Agincourt by English authors; the name of the village is now Azincourt.

Isabeau de Bavière (1371–1436). The king, Charles VI *le Bien-aimé* (1380–1422), suffered from recurring fits of madness that lasted months at a time, during which the queen had full power as regent of the kingdom. It was during one of these periods of the king's madness that Isabeau recognized, in a sense, the claims of the English king. The treaty of Troyes specified that Henry V of England (1399–1422) would marry Catherine, daughter of Charles VI and Queen Isabeau, that their expected son would inherit the crown of France at the death of Charles VI, and that he would reign over the two distinct kingdoms of England and France. The Salic law would be ignored. By virtue of this agreement the crown of France would not go to Charles VI's only living son, Charles, even though he had used the title of dauphin since the death of his brother Louis de Guyenne in 1415. Since 1343 the sovereignty of the province of Dauphiné and the title of dauphin were prerogatives of the male heir to the throne. By the treaty of Troyes the dauphin was disinherited and banished from the court: the treaty called him "the pretended dauphin." The official motivation for his disinheritance was his alleged conspiracy to have the duke of Burgundy murdered: Jean *Sans-peur* (1371–1419)[3] had been killed by some of the dauphin's associates during an interview with the dauphin on the bridge at Monterau.

Naturally enough, the dauphin denied the validity of the treaty of Troyes. He set up residence in central France on the Loire river in territories that supported him against his mother, the king of England, and the duke of Burgundy, the most powerful vassal of the king of France, who was bent on revenge for the murder of his father and who expected to gain more influence by recognizing the double monarchy. While he never had the build and demeanor of a fighter, the dauphin was able to organize an effective resistance. In 1422, as soon as he heard of the death of his father, Charles VI, he was proclaimed and anointed king by Regnault de Chartres, archbishop of Reims, who was also his chancellor and resided at the court. But since Reims was in Burgundian hands, the venue chosen for the coronation was the

---

[3]The dauphin was not a party to the murder, which was itself done in revenge for the assassination of Louis d'Orléans in 1407.

cathedral of Poitiers. The dauphin's supporters were named after the comte Bernard d'Armagnac, who had been assassinated in Paris by the partisans of the duke of Burgundy when the duke entered the city.

The dauphin obtained the services of mercenaries sent by the duke of Milan, Filippo Visconti (1391–1447), whose sister, Valentina (1364–1408), had been married to Charles d'Orléans. He also gained the support of the Parliament of Scotland, which sent him some seven thousand soldiers, later reinforced by some ten thousand under the command of Archibald, fourth earl of Douglas. After a victory at Beaugé (March 21, 1421), however, the Scots were decimated by the duke of Bedford at Verneuil (August 7, 1424).[4]

Jeanne's Home Country

Jeanne's home village, Domremy, was a few hundred yards on the left bank of the river Meuse, which in that area marked the border with the duchy of Lorraine and which was also the frontier with the Holy Empire of the German Nation. Immediately to the east were the lands of the duke of Lorraine, Charles II *le Hardi* (1390–1431). In the south the ducal lands were likewise quite near: the town of Neufchâteau was in the duchy in spite of the king of France's ineffective claim that it belonged to him.

But the duchy was not the whole of Lorraine. In the north and west, roughly, there were the three bishoprics of Metz, Toul, and Verdun, whose bishops were temporal lords for large sections of their dioceses. In the west also there was the county (soon the duchy) of Bar, created three centuries before through the marriage of Comte Louis de Mousson and Sophie de Luxembourg.[5] The comte de Bar was vassal to the emperor for his

[4]The earl of Douglas was killed in the battle; so were his son James and John, earl of Buchan, the winner of Beaugé.

[5]She was a daughter of Duke Frédéric II of Luxembourg. Count Henri III was a prisoner of Philippe *le Bel* of France when he agreed to the treaty of Bruges (June 4, 1301), by which he recognized the suzerainty of the king of France for his lands west of the Meuse river. The *comté* de Bar was promoted to *duché* by the king in 1354.

lands on the right bank of the Meuse and, since 1297, to the king of France for those on the left bank. The lands of Bar and Lorraine were divided between the ecclesiastical jurisdictions of the three bishops.

There was no immediate reason for the duke of Lorraine to be involved in the French struggle. He owed no allegiance to the king of France but only to the emperor of the Holy Roman Empire of the German Nation. Yet over the centuries the ties of Lorraine with the empire, in the bishoprics, in the county of Bar, and in the duchy, were getting looser. With France there were long-lasting linguistic ties. The duchy was divided in three *baillages,* or bailiwicks, one of which, the *baillage d'Allemagne,* adjacent to the Germanic duchy of Deux-Ponts (Zweibrucken), was mostly German speaking. Likewise, the bishopric of Metz was invisibly cut in two by a linguistic border between French and German dialects. But French was the language of the reigning family and of the court at Nancy. There were matrimonial ties, as men and women of the nobility frequently married French subjects. The duchy being relatively small, noblemen from Lorraine were often at the service of the king of France, though others served the emperor. No one could forget that Duc Raoul himself (d. 1346) had been killed at the battle of Crécy, fighting with the French against the English.[6] Still less could one forget, in the county of Bar, that in 1415 Count Edouard III and two of his brothers were slain at the battle of Azincourt fighting the English.[7] Cleverly exploiting the tightening ties of blood, commerce, and culture between the kingdom of France and the three components of Lorraine, the kings intervened more and more frequently and more or less openly in the bishoprics of Metz, Toul, and Verdun, as also in the county of Bar and the duchy of Lorraine. Groups

[6]It was chiefly with Duke Raoul that the policy of the duchy of Lorraine turned toward the kingdom of France. The duchess Marie de Blois was a niece of King Philippe *le Bel.* Raoul's father, Ferri IV *le Lutteur* (1282–1329), who had a German wife, had been more involved in the affairs of the empire. In 1322 he was captured at Mühldorf by the troops of Louis of Bavaria, the successful claimant to the emperorship, when he was fighting alongside his brother-in-law, Friedrich *der Schöne* (1289–1330), Herzog of Oesterreich and Steiermarck.

[7]Edouard had succeeded his father in 1411.

of citizens in some of the cities sought and obtained official pa-
tronage by the king, although this had little immediate effect.
Yet both the dukes of Lorraine and the counts of Bar realized
that above all they needed good relations with Burgundy for the
obvious reason that their lands cut those of the duke of Burgundy in two. They could not afford to antagonize this powerful neighbor whose subjects and troops periodically had to cross
through Lorraine as they traveled back and forth between Burgundy proper and the Netherlands.

Domremy was itself divided politically between the county
of Bar south of a narrow creek and the royal land in the *baillage*
of Chaumont north of it. The county's capital, Bar, lay some
fifty-four kilometers northwest. Jacques Darc's house was located in royal land between the creek and the church, extremely
close to both the county of Bar and the duchy of Lorraine. Only
because the king of France had at the time direct authority over
them could Charles VII, on July 31, 1429, while he was in
Château-Thierry on the way to Reims, exempt the inhabitants of
the twin villages of Domremy and Greux from taxation in per-
petuity. This part of the direct royal domain, centered on the
town and fortress of Vaucouleurs, had formerly belonged to the
county of Bar. It had been ceded to the king in the early fourteenth century, one hundred years before the time of Jeanne *la
Pucelle*. On January 25, 1571, it would be given back to the
duke of Lorraine and Bar by Charles IX of France (1550–1574,
king in 1560). When the area was turned over to the duchy, the
villages lost their tax exemption, since the king's decrees were
without legal value beyond the borders of the kingdom. They recovered it when the duchies became officially French at the death
of their last sovereign.[8] They finally lost it when it was abolished
by the French Revolution as an unwarranted privilege.

---

[8]This was the exiled king of Poland, Stanislas Leszczinski
(1677–1766), who had been made duke of Lorraine in 1737 through the
influence of his son-in-law, Louis XV of France. The last traditional duke,
François III (1708–1765), had never lived in the duchy he had inherited in
1729; he abdicated in 1736 when he married Marie-Thérèse of Austria; he
became emperor of Austria, the first of the Hapsbourg-Lorraine line, in
1745.

Because of Domremy's location a few authors have argued that Jeanne was not a Lorrainer, or that she was a *Champagnarde,* her father having presumably been born in the town of Ceffonds in the county of Champagne. Nonetheless, the term "Lorraine" traditionally designates the lands that came under the spiritual leadership of the medieval bishops of Metz, Toul, and Verdun or, in the ecclesiastical reorganization made in the eighteenth century, of the modern dioceses of Metz, Nancy-Toul, Verdun, and St. Dié.[9]

Chaos in the Land

When Jeanne was old enough to understand what the adults were talking about, the county of Bar was ruled by the only surviving brother of Edouard III, Cardinal Louis de Bar, bishop of Châlons since 1413, who had, irregularly since he was a priest, succeeded him on the throne. One of the cardinal's nieces was Yolande d'Aragon (1380–1442), daughter of his sister Yolande de Bar and the king of Aragon, Juan I (1350–1396). Yolande d'Aragon had married the duke of Anjou, Louis II (d. 1417), and their daughter Marie was the queen of France. On Yolande's advice the cardinal officially adopted one of her sons, René d'Anjou (1408–1480), who succeeded him as comte de Bar, René I, in 1430. Through his father René d'Anjou was also comte de Provence and heir to the kingdom of Sicily. When his mother died in 1440 he claimed the kingdom of Aragon.[10] The dauphin was his brother-in-law. His wife, Isabeau de Lorraine (d. 1453), was the daughter of Duke Charles II. At their marriage

[9]The area of the Vosges mountains around St.-Dié had been officially part of the diocese of Toul, but it included several renowned abbeys—Senones, Moyenmoutier, Etival—that were practically free from episcopal supervision. As regards ecclesiastical jurisdiction, the ducal lands were divided between the three dioceses, which all came under the metropolitan authority of Trèves. The concordat of 1804 between Napoléon and Pius VII placed them under the archbishop of Besançon. After the Franco-Prussian war of 1870 the diocese of Metz, like that of Strasbourg in neighboring Alsace, was exempted from metropolitan authority.

[10]René was not able to reign over Sicily or Aragon. He spent his later years in the county of Provence.

the settlement specified that through his wife he would inherit the duchy of Lorraine at his father-in-law's death, for the Salic law had no legal standing in Lorraine.[11] The prospect of this inheritance was an additional convincing reason why the count of Bar wished to keep good relations with the duke of Burgundy.

Jeanne, however, paid no attention to anything that looked like petty maneuvering. When she was invited to Nancy by the duke of Lorraine in the winter of 1428–29, she expressed the hope that René would support her cause.[12] René had indeed fought the English party when he was attacked in January 1427 by Jean de Vergy. He was on that occasion assisted by Robert de Baudricourt. But his uncle the cardinal, who was still administering the county, was also secretly negotiating with the Burgundian and English parties. On April 13, 1429, the cardinal acknowledged the claims of the English king. On May 6, two days before the English commanders gave up the siege of Orléans, René allied himself officially with the duke of Bedford.[13]

[11]The duke had sons from his concubine Alison May, but they could not inherit the duchy because they were not legitimate. At the duke's death the unfortunate Alison May was dragged through the streets and lynched by the people of Nancy.

[12]While she was waiting in Vaucouleurs for the governor, Robert de Baudricourt, to send her to Chinon with an escort, Jeanne was invited by the duke of Lorraine, and she rode to Nancy with her mother's cousin Durand Laxart (Q. II, p. 444). The soldier Jean de Nouillonpont accompanied her as far as Toul, and she returned around the first Sunday in Lent, February 13, 1429 (Q, 2:437). Bertrand de Poulengy reported that on the way to Nancy she went on pilgrimage to St.-Nicolas-de-Port (Q, 2:457). Vaucouleurs lies west of Nancy, and St.-Nicolas-de-Port is east, but one could easily reach St.-Nicolas by way of Pont-St.-Vincent, thus bypassing the capital of the duchy.

[13]John of Lancaster (1389–1435), duke of Bedford, was the third son of Henry IV of England. When his brother Henry V died in 1422 and the new king, Henry VI, was less than one year old, he became regent for the kingdom of France, his brother the duke of Gloucester being regent for the kingdom of England. Bedford strengthened the Burgundian alliance by marrying Anne de Bourgogne, sister of duke Philippe *le Hardi*. He was the political and military power behind the ecclesiastical façade of the Rouen tribunal. He regarded Jeanne as a tool of the devil, and his letter to the bishop of Beauvais specified that she would remain the king's prisoner if the tribunal did not find her guilty of heresy. According to Guillaume Colles

Yet he also attended the coronation of Charles VII on July 17, and on August 5 he withdrew his allegiance to Henry VI. Clearly, Duke René's timing was poor and his reading of the signs of the times careless. Unlike his mother, Yolande, he generally lacked political sense. Yet when Charles II died in Nancy in 1431 he became duke of the two duchies. The larger part of his lands lay in the empire, a small part west of the Meuse in the kingdom of France.

Nineteen kilometers to the north of Domremy, the city of Vaucouleurs and its immediate neighborhood belonged to no local sovereign. They were part of the kingdom of France, and since 1337 they were directly in the king's domains, being administered by a military commander appointed by the king. This was Robert de Baudricourt (d. 1454), a nobleman of Lorraine at the service of the dauphin, whose second wife, Alarde de Chambley, belonged to a noble family of the county of Bar.[14] The English were generally far enough from Vaucouleurs. More immediately threatening were the Burgundians, but so far the *capitaine* had managed to fence off their occasional forays in the land under his care. Yet after 1423, when Jacques d'Harcourt, a supporter of the dauphin, had been pushed out of Picardy by the earl of Warwick, the duke of Bedford resolved to reduce the cities and fortresses that were faithful to the dauphin along the eastern borders. Antoine de Vergy had been repelled, but there was no certainty that Vaucouleurs could withstand a more systematic assault.

The political divisions erected by several centuries of feudal rule enormously complicated the rather simple geography of the land. The Meuse flows from south to north between moderately high hills, following a course toward the Rhine that vaguely

---

the duke of Bedford watched from behind a curtain when Jeanne was examined for virginity by his wife and some other ladies. He died in Rouen and was buried in the sanctuary of the cathedral. In England itself the house of Lancaster was regarded by many as having usurped the throne. The attempt to obtain the throne of France may be seen as an extension of this usurpation. The War of the Roses, between the houses of Lancaster and York, was still to come. The house of York was destined to win.

[14]Alarde de Chambley was the widow of Jean de Manonville when she married Robert de Baudricourt.

parallels the course of the Moselle farther east. Beyond the Moselle there stretches a plateau that leads to the Vosges mountains. The continental climate was roughly what it still is today: very cold in winter with possible accumulations of snow, quite hot in summer and either dry or humid depending on whether the prevailing winds are from the east or the west.

To us today the political picture seems needlessly complex. But it looked much simpler to the people of those lands at that time. The mind-set was still feudal. Loyalty did not go to a nation but to a person—the baron, count, marquis, duke, king, or emperor—who was considered to have received dominion of the land by divine mandate. Presumably the peasants and small farmers who raised sheep, goats, and cattle, who tilled the fields and harvested their grains, who tended orchards and picked their fruits in the late summer paid little attention to the conflicts of the nobility as long as these did not interfere with their seasonal tasks and imperil their animals and their families. Yet they were aware of what was going on in the higher spheres of the social hierarchy, and they kept abreast of whatever events could affect their welfare. Jeanne knew in 1428–1429, from public rumor, that the son of Charles VII, barely five years old, was now engaged to Margaret of Scotland,[15] an engagement that sealed the dauphin's Scottish alliance. She told Jean de Nouillonpont: "No one in the world, neither kings nor dukes or daughter of the king of Scotland or others can recover the kingdom of France, and there is no help except from me, though I would prefer to stay with my poor mother, for that is not my estate. But I must go, and I will do it, because my Lord wants me to do it."[16] Jeanne also knew that the aging duke of Lorraine was not living with his wife, the holy Marguerite de Bavière, but with his mistress.[17]

Jeanne lived in a time of war. But it was a war with no front. At least in the outlying area of the kingdom along the border of the duchy of Lorraine fighting was no more than occasional. Roving bands came and went, usually living off the land

---

[15]The future Louis XI (1423–1483) married Margaret of Scotland when he reached the age of fourteen.

[16]Q, 2:436.

[17]The duke had married Marguerite de Bavière in 1393.

and plundering along the way. But what triggered Jeanne's indignation was the siege of Orléans. For it was a convention of feudal times that one would not attack a city whose lord, its vowed defender, was already a prisoner. And Charles d'Orléans, captured with many others at the battle of Azincourt on October 24, 1415, was still a prisoner in England. The decision to lay siege to Orléans was made by Thomas Montagu, earl of Salisbury, who commanded an army that had recently landed in France. Salisbury's opinion prevailed over that of Bedford, who wished to take Angers first. This was unfortunate for him, since he was killed by a stray cannonball in the first days of the siege. The decision was a breach of the code of knighthood, but the code was more and more ignored in the practice of war. In any case the siege was not complete, as it failed to block the entry of food and eventual reinforcements into the city. This was due in part to the English strategy that preferred open-air battles to waiting around a city and storming well-guarded walls, in part to the duke of Burgundy's sudden withdrawal of the contingent he had sent to assist his allies. Philippe *le Bon* wanted to have command of the city once it was taken. When this plan was rejected by the duke of Bedford, he ordered all Burgundians to abandon the siege. There was, all along, great activity, but the many skirmishes that took place before the reinforcements that brought Jeanne *la Pucelle* arrived were due to the fighting spirit of the defenders rather than to aggressive tactics on the part of the assailants.

Salisbury's successor, John Talbot, earl of Shrewsbury (ca. 1388–1453),[18] was not devoid of civility. In fact, he had friendly communications with the bâtard d'Orléans, future comte de Dunois, who defended the city in the name of his half brother Charles. The siege began on October 12, 1429. At Christmas Lord Talbot asked Dunois if he could borrow some minstrels to

---

[18]Talbot would be killed in the last battle of the Hundred Years' War, at Castillon, when he lost Bordeaux and the province of Guyenne to Charles VII. It is intriguing that the English victories of Crécy and Azincourt were due to the technical superiority of English archery, and their defeats around Bordeaux were brought about by the technical superiority of French artillery, which Charles VII had steadily built up.

help in the celebration of the birth of Christ. And so several French musicians spent part of the day singing carols for the assailants. On another occasion, on February 22, 1430, the earl of Suffolk, William de la Pole, sent a messenger to Dunois with a "dish filled with figs, grapes, and dates" and a request asking in return for "black pigskin to line a robe, which he did willingly."[19]

Chaos in the Church

The Church in the first half of the fifteenth century was in no better shape than the kingdom of France. In principle, the solution to the problem of the Great Schism had been found. As the century opened there had been two popes, Boniface IX (1389–1404) in Rome and Benedict XIII (1394–1423) in Avignon. In an attempt to end the schism between Benedict and Boniface's second successor, Gregory XII (1406–1415), the Council of Pisa had declared Benedict a heretic on June 5, 1409. But instead of rallying to Gregory it had elected the Franciscan Pierre de Candie (ca. 1340–1415) as Alexander V on June 26. In 1410 the Council of Basle elected John XXIII (1410–1415) to succeed Alexander. John XXIII moved to Avignon. After complicated diplomatic maneuvers and some military endeavors Benedict XIII took refuge in Spain with a handful of cardinals. Abandoned by most of his former supporters, he still thought that he was the only legitimate pope. Before his death he therefore created four cardinals, who elected Clement VIII in 1425. Meanwhile, in 1415 the Council of Constance had obtained the resignation of the other two rival popes, John XXIII and Gregory XII. In 1417 it had deposed Alexander V. The main group of cardinals had then elected Martin V (1417–1431) as successor to all three. He took up residence in Rome.

Yet the papacy was still divided. Clement VIII resigned on July 26, 1429. But in 1425 another rival, Benedict XIV (1425–1430), had been elected in Spain—though by one cardinal only!—as Benedict XIII's true successor. Kings, princes, free cities, and their bishops continued therefore to be divided in their papal allegiances. Martin V had the largest obedience, and

[19]The story is told in *Journal du siège d'Orléans:* Q, 2:131.

Benedict XIV found little support. Yet Clement VIII generally had the loyalty of the French and the Scots. One could still argue that the Avignon line was legitimate, all the popes having resided in that city, under French protection yet outside the kingdom of France, from 1309 to 1377. And even during the ensuing papal schism the popes of Avignon were not undistinguished.

In order to safeguard the unity of the Church it was necessary to restore the unity of the papacy. With this in view the conviction had grown among theologians and canon lawyers that a general council must be able to decide who is the true Bishop of Rome, and to that effect it must have the capacity to depose those it would not endorse. Logically this implied that, at least in certain circumstances, a general council has authority over the single Bishop of Rome. The relative authority of general councils and the Bishop of Rome had therefore become a matter of public debate, especially in the universities.

Conciliarism was the theory that a general council of the Church is superior to the pope. Indeed, the solution that was brought by the Council of Constance to the multiple papacy of the time was based on conciliarism. Yet convictions could easily waver. Martin V, elected on a conciliaristic principle, rejected it as soon as it was safe to do so. The distinguished Renaissance figure, Aeneas Sylvius Piccolomini (d. 1464), was a determined conciliarist until 1458, when he was elected Bishop of Rome. As Pius II, he found himself to be a staunch papalist!

Jeanne and the people of Domremy, however, must have had little or no knowledge of the latest trends in theological thought and of the shifting papal loyalties of princes and cardinals.

Deep Spirituality

Like other periods of political instability and religious uncertainty, the early fifteenth century was not devoid of deep spirituality. The mystical schools of the Dominicans Johannes Tauler (ca. 1300–1361) and Heinrich Suso (1296–1366), which had flourished on both sides of the Rhine, were still influential. Informal groups of "Friends of God" encouraged one another in the ways of the inner life. Along the lower Rhine there was developing among the Brethren of the Common Life a *devotio*

moderna that was, with Jan van Ruysbroeck (1293–1381), open
to mystical union with God, and centered, with Thomas à Kem-
pis (ca. 1380–1471), on the imitation of Christ and the euchar-
istic presence. Its warm meditative approach to Jesus, its
sacramental emphasis, and its reasonable asceticism were easily
accessible to lay persons.

In addition, the preaching of the friars, especially Franciscans (St. Bernardine of Siena, d. 1444) and Dominicans (St. Vin-
cent Ferrer, d. 1419) but also Augustinians and Carmelites, was
widely popular. Franciscans especially advocated a constant invocation of the name of Jesus that brought a form of contemplation to the level of ordinary people. Not by accident or personal
fancy did the bishop of Toul, in whose jurisdiction lay the village
of Domremy, commonly choose a *Cordelier* (from one of the
branches of the Order of St. Francis) as his auxiliary. In 1422
Henri de Vaucouleurs, guardian of the *Cordeliers* of Toul, was
made titular bishop of Chrysopolis and auxiliary of Henri de
Ville, bishop of Toul.[20] The *Cordelier* friars of Neufchâteau often
preached in the neighboring countryside, and not only in the
duchy of Lorraine. They easily went on preaching tours in the
county of Bar and the captaincy of Vaucouleurs.

In these conditions it was not utopian for lay people who
felt so inclined to have access to the most advanced spirituality
formulated in simple terms. A good practice of the inner life, if
not always accompanied by theoretical knowledge, was not the
privilege of the clergy and the educated laity. Nor did it flourish
only in monasteries. The great women mystics of the thirteenth
and fourteenth centuries continued to be influential through
their writings, the retelling of their lives, and the explanation of
their teachings. Admittedly resistance to the spiritual leadership
of women was frequent, especially among bishops, who tended
to be all too jealous of their authority. Yet there were still,
though not in Lorraine, abbesses with quasi-episcopal jurisdiction. It was by no means unusual for women to be acknowledged
instruments of the Spirit of God. Brigid of Sweden (ca.
1303–1373) and Catherine of Siena (ca. 1347–1380) had not
hesitated, in the name of God, to urge Gregory XI (1331–1378,

---

[20]Marot, *Jeanne*, 35.

pope in 1370) to bring the papacy back from Avignon to Rome. Women mystics were presumably far from rare, though most of them would not be generally known, since the interior life as such does not belong to the public domain.

Jeanne's Contemporaries

Jeanne was contemporary with the Italian Francesca da Busso (1383–1440), a married lady, later known as St. Francesca Romana, who founded the Oblates of St. Frances and entered their community on the death of her husband, Lorenzo dei Ponziani. Catherine of Bologna (1423–1463), a Poor Clare in Ferrara and Bologna, would be known as an artist in manuscript illuminations and an author who exploited the traditional image of the spiritual battle.[21] Jeanne's life also overlapped with that of the English recluse Julian of Norwich (ca. 1373–after 1433). It easily fit the life of another mystic of England, Margery Kempe (ca. 1373–ca. 1440), who made pilgrimage her way of life after leaving her husband at their home in Norfolk. Another contemporary, Elizabeth of Schiedam (d. 1433), was, like Jeanne, suspected of witchcraft. In Lorraine itself the neglected wife of the duke, Marguerite de Bavière, led a life of devotion and good works and would later be honored as a saint.

In the kingdom of France at the very time of Jeanne, Colette de Corbie (1381–1447) was traveling through the land actively reforming the Order of St. Clare and opening new communities. She was to enjoy the active protection of Charles VII's successor, his often rebellious son Louis XI (1423–1483). Colette and Jeanne happened to be in the same city, Moulins, in November 1429. Colette was at a monastery she had established there in 1422. Jeanne arrived in the town around November 5 after the easy liberation of St. Pierre-le-Moûtier, thirty-one kilometers to the north. She departed for the unsuccessful siege of La Charité-sur-Loire, which began on November 25. But there is no evidence that they met or even that they knew of each other.[22]

[21]She wrote *Le Sette Arme necessarie alla battaglia spirituale* (1438).
[22]Mme. Ste-Marie Perrin, *St Colette and Her Reform: A Page from the History of the Church* (London: Sands & Co., 1923) 197–210. St. Colette was Colette Boylet, born near Corbie.

By the nature of their respective missions there is a better chance that Colette knew about Jeanne than the reverse. Jeanne had some familiarity with Franciscans, since their preachers radiated from Neufchâteau, but she had never been exposed to religious sisters. There was no convent in the vicinity of Domremy. The nearest houses of Poor Clares were in Toul and Nancy. Once she started on her task regarding Orléans and Reims, Jeanne did frequent the homes of ladies of the bourgeoisie and the nobility, where she often spent the night or stayed for a few days. But there is no evidence that she ever visited nunneries.[23]

Along with her family and her village the young Jeannette was caught in the turmoils of an unsettled society. It was all too common for small peasants to experience poverty. They also knew anxiety and at times destitution when marauders raided the area. So it happened in 1425, when the cattle of Domremy and Greux were stolen by a band led by a certain Henri d'Orly. The cattle were recovered, for Henri d'Orly was pursued and eventually put to death by the powerful comte de Vaudémont, Antoine (d. 1458), a nephew of the duke of Lorraine, Charles II.[24] Again in July 1428 the villagers and their flocks had to run away when Jean de Vergy was threatening the town of Vaucouleurs. They found shelter over the border at Neufchâteau while the village, including the church, was set on fire.[25] Jeanne and her family stayed at Neufchâteau some two weeks[26] in the house of a certain

---

[23]That Jeanne was a Franciscan tertiary is a bizarre hypothesis that has no foundation in any document. It is based on another hypothesis: Jeanne would have been educated in her mission by emissaries of the Third Order Franciscans (who would be her "voices") acting under the orders of Yolande d'Aragon and Colette de Corbie! See a description of this alleged Franciscan conspiracy in Sermoise, *Les Missions,* passim.

[24]Antoine de Vaudémont would vainly lay claim to the crown of Lorraine at the death of his uncle against the claims of Charles II's daughter and son-in-law René d'Anjou. But the Salic law was not recognized in Lorraine, and the ducal crown could be held and transmitted by women.

[25]Beatrice d'Estellin: Q, 2:396.

[26]2/22: T, 1:46; Jeanne herself gives the name or nickname of the woman in whose house they were lodged: *la Rousse.* According to Jean Moreau, however, they stayed there only four days, Q, 2:392.

Jeanne *la Rousse*. At Rouen the judges would claim that this woman ran a drinking place, and they accused Jeanne of leading a dissolute life with "young loose women."[27]

Like girls in all of human history, Jeanne had to deal with the matrimonial customs of the age, though she did not become their victim. At one point her parents tried to get her married, possibly after her father had dreams in which he saw her go away with soldiers. Using their customary prerogative, they must have promised her to a young man. As she admitted at her trial, Jeanne was summoned to appear before the ecclesiastical tribunal of the bishop of Toul. In Rouen the lawyer, Jean de la Fontaine, had wrong information: he thought that she had lodged a complaint against the man. Jeanne corrected him. The plaintiff was the man, who was suing her for breach of promise to marry.[28] But she herself had made no such promise, and the tribunal found her innocent of the charge. When this happened the voices were already talking to Jeanne. Before she went to Toul they assured her that she would win the case. She must have been thirteen or fourteen, girls being marriageable at twelve. Some authors have placed this episode during the stay at Neufchâteau, but this cannot be correct. A sojourn of four days or even of two weeks would not have given enough time for Jeanne to seem to be engaged to a young man, for this man to sue her for breach of promise of marriage, and for the officials of Toul to send their summons. In any case, Jeanne could not have traveled to Toul when roads and paths were made dangerous by Jean de Vergy's expedition.

Of the turmoils in the Church, meantime, Jeanne seems to have known very little. The problems of the papacy were hardly a topic for popular preaching. And if the powerful could for some time choose their pope among two or three claimants the ordinary people were scarcely affected by their choices. Yet Jeanne could not escape some ecclesiastical dilemmas when the ecclesiastics were divided. Pierre Cauchon de Sommièvre (d. 1440), the bishop of Beauvais who found her guilty and had her

---

[27]This was article 8 in a list of seventy articles of accusation (T, 1:200), but it was not kept in the later list of twelve articles.

[28]3/12: T, 1:123, 127.

burned, was at the same time a determined partisan of the English succession to the crown of France and a supporter of the pope who was in Rome against his rivals. In 1430 and 1431 he was bent on destroying the main cause of the recent defeats of English power. Jeanne, in fact, agreed with him regarding the pope. But they were at odds in politics. And the bishop made no secret of his determination to destroy her, for he assured her: "The king has ordered me that I proceed to your trial and I will do it."[29]

[29]Massieu: Q, 3:154.

TWO

A Girl with No Name

Naturally she may be called Jeanne d'Arc. This has been the custom for several centuries. But one cannot be sure it was her name. At the first public audience of her trial in Rouen on February 21, 1431, the president of the tribunal, Bishop Cauchon de Sommièvre, told her to give her "name and surname." She gave only the diminutive by which she was commonly known in her village: "At home I was called Jeannette. Since my coming to France, Jeanne. I do not know my surname."[1] Jeannette naturally stands for Jeanne, the name she received at baptism. It was the name of at least two of her godmothers—Jeannette, widow of Tiercelin Leclerc, and Jeannette Royer. From what she said she had an unspecified number of godmothers, others being Agnes, Sybil, and Beatrice. Two of her godfathers were Jean Ligné and Jean Barrey, and Beatrice d'Estellin also listed Jean Moreau, Jean Le Langart, and the late Jean Rainguesson among her godfathers.[2] There were thus converging reasons of spiritual kinship to have her christened Jeanne.

Jeanne Darc?

When asked for the names of her father and mother she responded, "My father was called Jacques Darc, my mother Isabelle." Her father had a surname, though we cannot be sure what it was exactly. In French it is given as Tarc,[3] or Darc, the c

[1] T, 2:40.
[2] Q, 2:395.
[3] T, 1:40.

19

being silent, pronounced with a wide open *a*, as is not unusual even today in the parlance of Lorraine, or also as Day or d'Ay, with a diphthong.[4] In fifteenth-century spelling, Darc or d'Arc would be the same. Originally it may have designated someone who was issued from a village called Arc, the *c* being again mute. Arc-en-Barrois lies some sixty kilometers southwest of Dom-remy. Even though Jeanne's father most probably came from Ceffonds in Champagne, his family may have originated in Arc-en-Barrois.[5]

There was, one should add, a family Darc that was living in Paris in the first decade of the century. In 1407 a certain Jeanne Darc was known in the entourage of King Charles VI: on June 12 she was paid eighteen sols for delivering flower wreaths to the royal residence of Hôtel St.-Pol in Paris.[6] That a branch of the family would have settled in Paris with some sort of flower business and another in Domremy to work a small farm for a living is entirely possible.

Jeanne Romée?

Jeanne gave no surname for her mother. Isabelle, itself a variant of Elizabeth, was sufficient. Yet later in the course of the trial she revealed her mother's surname. On March 24 in an interrogation that took place in her prison cell she corrected the minute that was being read to her and specified that her own surname was either Darc (as above) or Romée (Rommée), this being her mother's surname, but that it was customary in her village for girls to take their mother's name.[7] Clearly, Jeanne knew what a surname was for an individual, but she had yet no notion

[4]As in the decree of ennoblement of Jeanne's family, where these last two forms are used. These variants reflect differences of pronunciation of the name. In addition there would be no difference in the fifteenth century between Darc and d'Arc, Day or d'Ay. Nobility comes from ancestry or from royal decree, not from a particle before a name.

[5]Other villages have been suggested such as Ars-sur-Moselle, Art-sur-Meurthe, the pronunciation being the same as that of Arc.

[6]Photocopy of a document preserved in the Archives Nationales in Paris, in Pierre de Sermoise, *Les Missions,* after p. 96.

[7]T, 1:181.

of one that would designate a family, and for herself she was not sure which of her parental surnames she ought to claim.

The practice of having family names, which was common in Roman civilization, had been lost in Gaul with the barbarian invasions, as it was not a custom of the Germanic tribes that came from over the Rhine at the end of the fifth century. Surnames had begun to be adopted in France about two centuries before Jeanne's time in the reign of Philippe II, generally known as Philippe Auguste (1180–1223). Formerly, outside of the nobility with its many titles taken from ancestors or from the land, ordinary people were simply called by their baptismal name, a clarification being easily added when necessary to avoid confusion by specifying the name of the father, on the model of Simon bar Jonas, "Simon, son of John." In rural areas, however, customs change slowly. Men, it would seem, took a name before women, presumably because it was useful for public transactions and not particularly relevant inside the home or on the farm.

In any case, Isabelle's name may be quite significant: Rommée or, rather, Romée. Spelling fluctuated widely before the invention of printing—that was made a few years later, in 1440, in the neighboring German lands—began a slow movement toward uniformity. Yet one *m* makes better sense than two, for presumably Romée designates someone who has traveled to Rome, in other words, a pilgrim. Isabelle of course may never have visited Rome, though this is not excluded. The name may have come to her from an ancestor who had. Unless, but this is a suggestion of my own and not found in any writing about Jeanne, the name Romée has another origin and meaning. It is not impossible that in the part of France Isabelle came from Romée would have been a variant of *roumi*. The Larousse dictionary informs me that *roumi* is "the term by which the Arabs designate a Christian."[8] This may well be true. But in the popular language of Lorraine the term has also designated Gypsies, nomads who appear from time to time in small groups, stay for a while, and then pass on in their periodic roamings. Like its more common equivalent, *romanichel,* the term derives from the

[8] *Petit Larousse* (1959) art. *Roumi,* 932.

tzigane word *romani,* by which Gypsies, or some of their tribes, designate themselves.[9] The term may have inspired the popular belief, right or wrong, that they originally came from Romania.[10] In this case, Isabelle Romée may have been of remote Gypsy origin or, metaphorically, of a family where someone at one time was thought to behave like a Gypsy, perhaps because he or she was often absent on pilgrimage.

In keeping with the matrilineal custom of her village Jeanne ought to be known as Jeanne Romée rather than Jeanne Darc, of which later ages made Jeanne d'Arc, largely because the letter *d'* (from) in front of the name rather than in it tends to suggest a nobility that one is today less likely to read in a name like Darc.[11]

La Pucelle

Jeanne, however, called herself neither Romée nor Darc. When on June 2, 1429, the king sent the duke d'Alençon and herself to lay siege to the town of Jargeau on the Loire, he granted her next of kin the use of the name du Lys, with a coat of arms: an upward sword, silver, between two gold *fleurs-de-lys,* with a crown around it at midpoint of the blade, on azure background. Since *fleurs-de-lys* were featured on the royal arms it was a singular honor to include them in the du Lys arms. The name may also have delicately underlined Jeanne's connection with Orléans, for the message carriers employed by this city were officially known as Fleur du Lys and Coeur du Lys.[12] Yet unlike her brothers Pierre and Jean, Jeanne never used the name. This tallies perfectly with a response she gave on March 10: "She answers that she has never had a coat of arms; but her king gave one to her brothers."[13] The king did it on his own, to please

---

[9]*Romani* is itself a compilation of two tzigane words, *rom* and *manusch,* both of which designate human beings.

[10]Similarly, "gypsy" relates to Egypt, and "bohemian" to Bohemia. Another equivalent term that is used in French, *tsigane,* does not relate to an assumed place of origin.

[11]Yet see above, note 4.

[12]This point is emphasized by Gérard Pesme, *Jehanne,* 220–221.

[13]T, 1:114.

them, without any revelation or any petition from herself, in recognition of their services, since Jeanne's brothers had volunteered to serve in their sister's military escort, which they had joined before the march on Orléans. Jean du Lys and Pierre du Lys Jeanne's brothers could be if they wished. She remained in her own eyes and in those of her military companions what angels and saints called her, Jeanne *la Pucelle,* daughter of God.

Jeanne's Self-Identity

As Jeanne was vague about her name, so was she concerning her age. To the judges she declared that she was "nineteen years old, or thereabouts, as it seems to her."[14] On the basis of this declaration, but taking nineteen as the exact number of her years, the year 1412 has been assigned to her birth. The Epiphany, January 6, has been added because it is mentioned in a letter addressed on June 21, 1429, shortly before the coronation at Reims, by a gentleman from the court, Perceval de Boulainvilliers, to the duke of Milan, Filippo Visconti.[15] Yet this is hardly a valid proof of the date, for the same letter provides details that are clearly fanciful:

> In the night of the Lord's epiphanies, when people are wont joyfully to remember the deeds of Christ, she enters the realm of mortals and all the people of the place are moved by an extraordinary joy and, not knowing the birth of *la Pucelle,* run hither and thither, seeking what new thing has happened. The hearts of many felt a new joy. What more? Roosters, as though singers of new joy, broke into unheard of songs at an unusual time and, beating their wings, for nearly two hours they seemed to announce the happening of something new.[16]

[14]T, 1:41.

[15]Filippo Visconti was the younger brother of Valentina Visconti, wife of Louis II d'Orléans and mother of Charles d'Orléans. Their father was Galeazzo Visconti (1347–1402), duke of Milan, to whom Filippo succeeded after the murder of his elder brother Giovanni. Filippo was obviously interested in the fortunes of the duke of Orléans, and all the more so as his sister Valentina was next in succession to his duchy of Milan.

[16]Q, 5:116. The whole letter is on pages 114–21. "She enters this realm of mortals" translates *hanc intrat mortalium lucem.* It is a crude error

Neither the year nor the day is certain. That Jeanne was able to handle horses and to ride like a man when she left Vaucouleurs would suggest that she was several years older. One of Jeanne's objections when the angel told her that she should "go to France" was that "she could not ride a horse."[17] That Jeanne must have been more than nineteen in 1431 tallies with the testimony of Hauviette, her childhood friend: Jeanne "was two or three years older than I, as it was said."[18] When she reported this, Hauviette was about forty-five. The witnesses from Domremy made their depositions in the village itself on January 28, 1456. This would place Hauviette's birth around 1411, and that of Jeanne in 1407 or 1408. In 1431 she would have been twenty-two or twenty-three.

In any case Jeanne did not draw her self-identity from her origin or from her age. Nor did she find it in man-made privileges that reflected the king's indebtedness to her. She drew her identity exclusively from her status as a young woman who, for spiritual reasons, has promised to herself and to God to remain a virgin: *Jeanne la Pucelle*. This was what the angel called her.[19] And, one may well ask, who should know one's true name better than angels? *La Pucelle* is the appellation by which she introduced herself when she met with King Charles in Chinon, and that is how she signed the letters she addressed to the English commander of the Les Tourelles fort at Orléans and even to the duke of Bedford, regent of France for the child king Henry VI (1421–1471, king in 1422), and commander-in-chief of the English soldiers on French soil. On the dauphin's side, likewise, the captains of the king's army, and presumably also the ordinary soldiers, called her Jeanne *la Pucelle*. The word means a female child, and by implication, a virgin, but it does not only mean that, as a glance to etymology easily shows. With its masculine counterpart, *puceau,* the term is not likely to derive from the Latin word *puella* (feminine of archaic *puellus,* "little boy,"

---

to translate "torchbearers going through the village" (Sermoise, *Les Missions,* 49) or "in the light of torches" (Pesme, *Jeanne,* 48).

[17]T, 1:48.
[18]Q, 2:417–18.
[19]T, 1:126.

which evolved into the more common term, *puer*; the word is itself cognate with *pullus, pulla,* the offspring, male and female, of quadrupeds). Rather, *puceau, pucelle* are more likely to be constructed not directly from the Latin but from the French word *puce* (Latin, *pulex*), "a flea." Used metaphorically, it designates a wee thing, something or someone tiny, of no manifest importance.

Spiritually, the lesson of Jeanne's name is clear. It is not the customs and decisions of creatures that determine who she is. A person is not defined by what she has inherited or obtained from society or even by concern for her own self. In remaining nameless, Jeanne spontaneously renounced the fundamental human need for self-assertion. In calling herself *la Pucelle,* she declared herself to be of no importance, a wee person in whom littleness and virginity converge. She does not offer her body to any taker because there is nothing to take. Jeanne does not belong to herself.

Yet the question of Jeanne's self-identity is not thereby resolved. That she was a peasant girl from a very small village must have influenced her character. Today's maps call the village Domrémy-la-Pucelle or, rather, in keeping with the more usual local pronunciation, Domremy-la-Pucelle, without an accent, her self-appellation having been added, obviously, in her honor. In her time it was simply Domremi or Domremy, without an accent. *Y* and *i* being interchangeable, the name signifies "Remi's domain," and it testifies to the popularity of St. Remi (437–533), the archbishop of Reims who had baptized Clovis, king of the Franks, into the Christian and Catholic faith on Christmas Day of 497. Another village with the same name, Domrémy-aux-Bois, is, as the crow flies, only some thirty-eight kilometers northwest of Domremy-la-Pucelle. In fact, in the western section of the diocese of Toul where the two Domrémys are located, one counts no less than thirty-five parish churches dedicated to St. Remi.[20]

---

[20]Marot, *Jeanne,* see map on page 5.

A Village Girl

Domremy's twin village on the north side, Greux, is distinguished from it by no more than a brook, *le ruisseau des Trois-Fontaines*. The two of them are located on a north-south axis between the cities of Neufchâteau in the duchy of Lorraine, eleven kilometers to the south, and Vaucouleurs in royal territory, nineteen to the north. In former times a major Roman way, remains of which are still visible near Vaucouleurs, ran by, linking the large city of Lyon in the south to the metropolis of Trèves in the north. The episcopal city of Toul lay thirty kilometers to the northeast. It was not in the duchy, since the prince-bishop of Toul was also the secular ruler of a part of his diocese, though his territorial jurisdiction covered a good part of the duchy. Ecclesiastically the county of Bar and the duchy of Lorraine were cut up between the dioceses of Metz, Toul, and Verdun. The vast Gothic cathedral of Toul, begun in the first part of the thirteenth century, was still under construction. It would be given its front porch and towers only at the end of the fifteenth century.

In his village Jacques Darc was a respected farmer, appreciated by the lords of Bourlémont, who owned the castle on an island on the Meuse river where the peasants from time to time took refuge. He must have owned some agricultural land and a few animals, including sheep. Yet though Jeanne certainly loved her village and its people, her horizon was much wider than the rural countryside of her native valley. Contrary to what later ages have imagined, she was not a shepherdess. She did not normally tend her father's animals: this was a job for boys. Occasionally, as she said, she helped watch the flocks or herds of the village, presumably when these were led to graze *en bandon*,[21] that is, in lands that are commonly owned by the village or have been placed at its disposal by their owner.

Jeanne looked indeed like a peasant girl when, dressed in her usual red skirt,[22] she approached the governor of Vaucouleurs

---

[21]An expression in use in villages of Lorraine. I heard it often and used it in my childhood.

[22]Jean de Nouillonpont: Q, 2:437; Bertrand de Poulengy: 456.

in December 1428[23] and explained to him why he must send her to the dauphin of France. Robert de Baudricourt treated her like one when he told her "uncle" to take her back to her father and box her ears.[24] A couple of months later, however, by the time Jeanne mounted her horse with the escort that would guide her to Chinon[25] at the end of February 1429, she had become something else. She was recognized as a volunteer, hopefully inspired by God, who was determined to serve militarily on behalf of the prince she considered the only legitimate claimant to the crown of France. In a sense, a human person is what she does. And what she did, in Jeanne's case as she saw it, was to fulfill a mission that traced the parameters of her destiny because it had been received from God.

Nonetheless, devoted as she was to this mission, Jeanne did not define herself by it. As she commonly described it, her God-given task would end after she had successfully lifted the siege of the city of Orléans and led the dauphin to a proper coronation in the cathedral of Reims in keeping with the immemorial custom of the French monarchy. Her task done, she herself, as she must have thought, would then remain what she already was, *la Pucelle*, "the Little One," "the Virgin."

Female

It might be attractive today to suggest that Jeanne gained her identity from her womanhood. Yet this was not the case. Indeed, some authors have ventured the suggestion that she was not a woman but a young man in disguise. This, however, runs

[23]Following the testimony of Bertrand de Poulengy, most accounts of Jeanne's life refer to two distinct visits to Vaucouleurs, in May 1428 and February 1429. I find convincing the argument in favor of one sojourn only in Vaucouleurs, which lasted from December 1428 to February 1429; see Marot, *Jeanne*, 51–58.

[24]Q, 2:444.

[25]The escort was made of two mounted soldiers, Bertrand de Poulengy and Jean de Nouillonpont (also called Jean de Metz), with one servant each, one archer, and the royal guide Colet de Vienne, who may have been sent from Chinon or was requisitioned by Robert de Baudricourt for the specific purpose of guiding her through dangerous territory.

so openly against the evidence that it deserves no more than a mention. The duke of Alençon, a dear companion-at-arms since they met at the royal court in Chinon, was very clear in his testimony at the nullity inquiry: "Sometimes in the army I lay down next to Jeanne and the soldiers *à la paillade* [in the straw], and sometimes I saw Jeanne preparing for the night, and sometimes I looked at her breasts, which were beautiful."[26] At the time the duke was himself a young man away from his own beautiful wife, to whom Jeanne had promised to bring him back safely.[27] Woman Jeanne was. Yet womanhood did not provide her identity.

Indeed, Jeanne was skilled at the tasks that women of the period commonly did at home. She was adept at needlework; and since Jacques Darc raised sheep, she could spin and handle the loom. She did not shun these works when on occasion she did spend time with women. This was especially the case when she lived with the two ladies of Luxembourg. After she was captured on May 23, 1429, around six in the afternoon by a man of the "lance" of the bâtard de Vandomme, she was an honored prisoner of Jean de Luxembourg (d. 1440) and stayed for about three months (May to July) at his castle of Beaulieu-en-Vermandois, from which she tried to escape by locking up the guards. She was then moved to his castle of Beaurevoir, which was the usual residence of his wife, Jeanne de Béthune, and his aunt Jeanne de Luxembourg. This wealthy and powerful unmarried lady, a sister of the late Waleran de Luxembourg (d. 1415), connétable of France, comtesse de Ligny and St.-Pol since 1420, was a godmother of Charles VII. She was favorable to the dauphin and tried to protect *la Pucelle*, who testified that the demoiselle[28] de Luxembourg demanded "that she be not handed over to the English."[29] It is likely that Jeanne de Béthune, whose first husband, Robert de Bar, had died with the French knights at Azincourt, also favored Charles VII. During the nearly four months of her sojourn at Beaurevoir (August to November) Jeanne shared their genteel leisure and conversation. She liked them. Yet

[26]Q, 3:100.
[27]Q, 3:96.
[28]*Domicella* in the Latin translation.
[29]As stated by Jeanne and noted by Jean d'Estivet in connection with article 16 of the seventy articles of accusation, T, 1:213.

when they offered her a lady's dress she declined to take it, for, as she said, she could not abandon her male garment without Our Lord's permission.[30] Jeanne's identity was defined neither by her enemies nor by her friends, neither by what she did nor by what she wore. It was in God alone.

As a vassal of the duke of Burgundy Jean de Luxembourg could hardly have contradicted the duke's policy if he had wished to do so. While his aunt was still alive he secretly negotiated with the duke of Bedford, through the services of Pierre Cauchon, for Jeanne's transfer to an English captivity. Yet Jeanne remained under his guard until she was handed over to the duke of Bedford at the castle of Le Crotoy, which the comte de Ligny had just inherited from his aunt. Jeanne de Luxembourg died at Beaurevoir on November 13, 1429. With her an effective protectress of *la Pucelle* disappeared, for it was only two days later that Jean de Luxembourg, who inherited her lands and titles, received the duke of Bedford's blood money in exchange for Jeanne herself.[31] Jeanne soon started on the roundabout itinerary that took her in November to Arras, Drugy near St.-Riquier, then to the late Jeanne de Luxembourg's castle of Le Crotoy, where she was handed over to English guards. She left Le Crotoy for Rouen on December 12, going through St.-Valéry-sur-Somme, Eu, Dieppe, arriving at Christmas time. Several witnesses affirmed that a special cage had been built for her. For some time before the trial started she was kept in the cage, chained to it by her neck, hands, and legs in a standing position.[32] This was, of course, calculated to break her will.

---

[30]T, 1:211; 213.

[31]Jeanne de Béthune could not oppose her husband. His brother, Louis de Luxembourg (d. 1443), bishop of Thérouanne, archbishop of Rouen in 1436, cardinal in 1440, chancellor of France for Henry VI, was a devoted partisan of the double monarchy. He was present at the burning of Jeanne and was seen shedding a few tears. He died in England as bishop of Ely.

[32]Q, 3:155. No one reported seeing Jeanne in the cage, but several witnesses affirmed that the cage remained in her prison cell. I find no reason to reject Massieu's assertion that Jeanne was kept in the cage before the trial opened. Charles VII's son and successor, Louis XI, acquired a dubious fame for keeping prisoners in similar cages. This would not be the only example of the duke of Bedford's cruelty toward *la Pucelle*.

On February 22, 1430, Jeanne was asked by her questioner, Master Beaupère, if in her youth she had learned some skills. "Yes," she answered, she had learned to sew and to spin: "For spinning and sewing I fear no woman in Rouen."[33] Yet what Jeanne was able to do, what she liked to do, the skills she had acquired, did not define her. She could enjoy these tasks, but she would not be bound to them or by them. She would not be defined by anything that was customary. When she found that one of the charges against her was that she did not perform the tasks of women, she protested: "The works that are proper to women? There are enough other women to do them."[34]

Transvestite

For practical reasons since she was going to ride horses, and for reasons of common sense since she was going to be day and night with soldiers, she adopted the male garment, including the heavy accoutrements of battle. She did not spurn the long robes and flashy adornments that marked the nobility of their wearers and made them easily recognizable to friend and foe alike. She was willing indeed to return to female dress if at least, as she declared time and again, she was so authorized by her voices. She was willing to change if she was taken to a church prison, where, according to the rule of the Inquisition, she would be guarded by women. At times she refused to change even to attend Mass; at other times she was willing to change, but only for Mass. In her prison cell, however, she was never left alone, since several English soldiers remained inside to watch her. There she would not leave her male clothes. She knew that as the habit does not make a monk, a skirt does not make a woman and trousers do not make a man. Indeed, commenting on article 3 in the list of accusations in which she was charged with wearing "unusual and indecent clothes," she declared, "I make no distinction between male garment and female garment to receive my Savior."[35] Again

[33]T, 1:46.
[34]Accusation: . . . *perseveranter recusare et cetera opera facere sexui muliebri convenientia.* . . . Response: *Et quantum ad alia opera muliebra dicit quod sunt satis aliae mulieres pro hiis faciendis* (T, 1:212–13).
[35]T, 1:208.

she insisted: "The garment is nothing; it is of minor importance."[36] In any case she had acted by the command of God, the angels, and the saints, as in everything else she had done.

Jeanne repeated on March 25: "This garment does not weigh on my soul; to wear it is not against the Church."[37] Moreover, her adoption of male dress had been approved by the learned clerics who examined her at Poitiers in March and April of 1429. This was her point when she urged the judges to look up "the book" in Poitiers.[38] The questions were not new; she had answered them to the satisfaction of the learned clerics at Poitiers. But as this book, the minutes of the investigation that was made at the dauphin's request, was at the time somewhere in the king's domain, appealing to it acted as a taunt for those who were acting for the king of England. In any case, Jeanne refused to be defined by what she was wearing, by what horses she mounted, or by what surroundings she found herself in, whether fashionable at the king's court, exciting in camps and bivouacs, amicable with the duke and the duchess d'Alençon, comfortable with the ladies of Luxembourg, or dismal in the castle of Rouen.

Illiterate

One may well admit that Jeanne was, by modern standards, ignorant. She never went to school. If indeed there was a school in the neighborhood village of Maxey in the duchy of Lorraine as some authors assert,[39] the chance is that girls would not have been sent to it. Their education took place at home, and it came from the adult women of the family. In any case, whoever attended a village school could not have learned much more than

[36]T, 1:75.

[37]T, 1:155.

[38]According to Gérard Pesme the "Book of Poitiers" was discovered in the Vatican Library by Cardinal Tisserand. Tisserand would have placed the document in secret archives where no reader could access it (Pesme, *Jeanne,* 123, 258–60). This is not believable. Tisserand, who was himself from Lorraine and presumably interested in Jeanne d'Arc, was a scholar: why should he have wished to hide an important historical document?

[39]Thus Sermoise, *Les Missions,* 52.

reading, writing, and speaking a fairly standard French rather than simply the local *patois* of the upper Meuse.

"Jeanne was simple and ignorant; she knew nothing, to my knowledge, except in the matter of war." Such was the opinion of Marguerite La Touroulde, her hostess at Bourges.[40] It is clearly exaggerated, for Jeanne had the skills of peasant women, and La Touroulde was a city woman. "I know neither *A* nor *B*," Jeanne said to two professors of theology who were sent by the dauphin to interrogate her.[41] Yet her relative ignorance did not entail on her part a feeling of inferiority. To the theologians of Poitiers she declared: "There is in Our Lord's books more than in yours."[42] The king's courtiers and the clerics of Poitiers as well as the learned members and attendants of the tribunal in Rouen would have been surprised had she known much more than the average untutored child of a small farmer. She certainly could neither read nor write.[43] She did learn to sign her name, perhaps with someone guiding her hand, to the letters she dictated. In religious matters her instruction was fairly standard. From her mother she had learned *Pater noster, Ave Maria,* and *Credo* in Latin, the liturgical language.[44] From often hearing them she must have known also the Latin responses to the Mass. She must have learned about the sacraments and their practice from the pastor of the village church, which, at the center of the village cemetery, stood next to her parents' home, on the right when facing the house.[45] Since she could not read the Scriptures, what she knew of them she had heard from the pulpit or from biblical

---

[40]Q, 3:87.

[41]Gobert Thibault: Q, 3:74.

[42]*Il y a ès livres de Notre Seigneur plus que ès vôtres* (Q, 3:86).

[43]That Jeanne could not read or write is called a "mistaken . . . notion, odd and beguiling" in Rankin and Quintal, *First Biography,* 81. But there is no evidence that she ever read anything, and there is evidence that she dictated her letters and that she needed assistance to sign documents.

[44]T, 1:41.

[45]The church was oriented to the east. In the sixteenth century the vaults were consolidated. In 1825 the orientation was reversed, so that one enters it today through the former sanctuary. The baptismal font dates from the fourteenth century, and it may well be where Jeanne was baptized (Marot, *Jeanne,* 95–96).

stories used for pedagogical purposes or from looking at the windows and paintings in the churches and chapels she visited, in which, as everywhere in Christendom, biblical scenes were commonly featured. Likewise, what she knew of the saints and their history came chiefly from their statues, from legends that were reported of them, and from popular practices of devotion.

As to what Jeanne knew of the complicated politics of the times, it could only derive from what she heard at home and in her village. How detailed this knowledge was there is no way to assess. But the main lines were clear: the land was being devastated by war between three contending parties, Armagnacs, Burgundians, and English, the last two being allied for the time being. The fight centered on the question, who should be the king of France: the disinherited dauphin or Henry VI of England, a mere child? Additionally one could wonder if the duke of Burgundy, the most powerful vassal of the king of France and himself of royal blood, ought to dictate royal policy. To the down-to-earth mind of small farmers in the extreme east of the kingdom the answers were self-evident: Let the king of England stay in England and the duke of Burgundy in Burgundy! But for the men and women of Domremy there was a more immediate concern than dynastic problems. For war meant looting soldiery who lived off the land in the course of their strategic movements, marauding bands of ruffians who took advantage of the general turmoil, and desolation in the countryside. This must have been Jeanne's first impression of war. At least on one occasion she knew the plight of refugees, when in July 1428 the whole village went south to find shelter over the border at Neufchâteau.

Jeanne thus appears to be without any tie to what normally attracts people: jobs, skills, achievements, knowledge, the passing fashions of the time. It is not that she was indifferent to them. Indeed, she appreciated the rich material of the clothes that were from time to time made for her; she liked the horses that she rode during the campaign; she even liked the company of the noble women she met: the young wife of the duke d'Alençon, the wife and the aunt of Jean de Luxembourg; she did not shirk the honored practice—however strange to us—of sharing a bed with her hostesses. Yet none of those things was essential to her. She did not define herself through creatures.

Again, what defined Jeanne in her own eyes was not embodied in success, victory, or glory any more than in capture, imprisonment, and the copious insults she received from Jean
d'Estivet, promoter of her trial. It was exclusively what she put
into the composite name she wanted to be known by, the name
that came to her from baptism, Jeanne, explained by the name
that was given by the angels. On March 12 Jean de la Fontaine
asked if truly her voices had called her "daughter of God, daughter of the Church, big-hearted girl."[46] She answered that yes,
"before the siege of Orléans and since then every day" they had
sometimes called her "Jeanne *la Pucelle,* daughter of God." Thus
Jeanne, the youngest daughter of a peasant, even if somewhat
well off, was a nobody in the eyes of the world. In herself also
she had no value in her own eyes. Yet in her intimate exchange
with the heavenly realm she realized that she was God's daughter, since the angelic voices said so. And she was wholly devoted
to the fulfillment of her God-given task as soon as she was aware
of it. The spiritual way of Jeanne Darc has thus its point of departure in a total disregard of everything that makes human beings proud. In her own eyes and for herself Jeanne is a
non-entity. But she is also God's little thing, the *pucelle* that God
created and chose as his daughter. This is what defines her and
gives her an unmistakable spiritual identity. The littleness of
Jeanne and her ensuing self-knowledge as God's daughter is precisely the ground for the virginity connoted by the appellation *la
Pucelle.*

There was a subtle irony in the situation Jeanne *la Pucelle*
faced as she raised her standard against the king of England and
his armies. In 1429 when she was led to Chinon, Henry VI was
only seven years old. A king since infancy, since he was less than
one year of age when his father, Henry V, died, he was still, in
terms of government, nobody. His uncles held the power, especially John, duke of Bedford, his regent for France. It would appear later that the young king had inherited some strands of his
maternal grandfather's madness. He suffered from it in a quiet
way, in moments when he was hardly aware of his surroundings

[46]T, 1:126.

and quite unable to govern. At such times, it would seem, Henry VI fell into an absorbing piety in which he paid no attention to and could not comprehend the affairs of state.

The dauphin himself was not exempt from minor sequels of his father's disease. Rather than madness or piety these took the form of temporary sloth, inability to reach a decision, depression perhaps. It must have been partly his awareness of such defects in his character that made him prefer slow diplomatic processes to the swift but hazardous decisions of combat. Facing the immaturity of his nephew the king of England, Charles VII opposed a steady stubbornness that verged on inertia. But he never was the silly playboy that authors of historical fiction have enjoyed describing. It was, in fact, a bold decision, though natural enough, to take the title of dauphin at the unexpected death of his brother Louis. It was bolder still to challenge his mother Queen Isabeau de Bavière and denounce the treaty of Troyes as invalid. It was equally courageous for the dauphin to take the title of king of France as soon as his father died, in 1422, and to have himself crowned in the cathedral of Poitiers,[47] though this was not the traditional place and it could not be done with the oil of the *sainte ampoule*. The dauphin was able to transform an innate inertia into a stubborn determination to negotiate rather than fight. Yet he fought with courage when it became necessary, as was the case for the reconquest of Normandy and Guyenne. Indeed, his methods were in the long run successful. He gained back his kingdom through alternances of diplomacy and military action. His hesitancy, slowness, and caution irritated Jeanne, and it often left his military commanders powerless. Yet posterity was not wrong to call him Charles *le Victorieux*.

Nephew and uncle, rivals in politics, shared the same biological burden. Had Charles VII known it at the time, this should have sufficed to allay his fears that he was not legitimate[48] and was only, as the treaty of Troyes called him, "the pretended

---

[47]The dauphin was at Mehun-sur-Yèvre, near Bourges, when news of his father's death reached him.

[48]It was rumored that he was an illegitimate child of Queen Isabeau and her brother-in-law Louis, duke of Orléans, but this may be doubted. The ill repute of the queen may have been undeserved, a popular reaction to her engineering of the treaty of Troyes.

dauphin." Into the lives of these two kings, a young man and a child who shared the misfortune of a heavy human inheritance, there entered Jeanne *la Pucelle,* whose youth was not defined by years but by familiarity with the angels of God.

THREE

A Girl with a Mission

The mission that Jeanne believed she had to fulfill had two aspects that were closely related in her mind yet were not of the same value, one of them being entirely subordinate to the other. It had a public dimension and a private, interior one. Because history deals with visible events historians have generally retained those of Jeanne's doings that were destined to the public domain. They have been primarily interested in the impact of her achievements on the history of the French monarchy and, by the same token, in the consequences of Jeanne's short career for the future of both the French and the English nations. Jeanne acted in an advisory capacity at the service of one of the two parties competing for the crown of France. Indeed, she began her public career by approaching the nearest French official, the captain of Vaucouleurs.

This part of Jeanne's actions has made her a political figure, even a symbol of national liberation. It is still celebrated as such every year in the French Republic, in principle on the anniversary of her death, May 30. It is not so apparent, although it is known to historians, that Jeanne *la Pucelle*'s public career placed her in a line of French women who, at one time or another, have been actively involved in the wars of their motherland. Before Jeanne there had been St. Geneviève (420–512). In 451 this holy woman persuaded the feared conqueror Attila not to enter the town of Lutèce (the nucleus of the later Paris). Attila withdrew, only to have his troops cut to pieces a few days later at the battle of the *champs catalauniques* by the combined armies of Mérovée, king of the Franks (d. 458), Theodoric, king of the Visigoths, who was killed in the fighting, and the Roman general Aetius (d.

454). Jeanne in turn inspired other women fighters, beginning with Claude des Armoises.[1] A few decades later, in 1472, a certain Jeanne Laisné (born 1454) participated in the defense of the city of Beauvais against the duke of Burgundy, Charles *le Téméraire* (d. 1474). The weapon she used with efficacy gained her the nickname, Jeanne *Hachette* (the Hatchet). And one could place along the line of these fighting women the numberless women who took an active part in the Resistance against the German occupation of France during World War II.

Yet Jeanne's mission had a more interior dimension, which would have remained unknown had she not revealed it. It came, as she attested, from God. Jeanne was aware of a call that she did not feel free to ignore, although she found it at first surprising and even frightening. Over the centuries it is chiefly this aspect of Jeanne's story that has struck popular imagination: she was a visionary, a privileged seer to whom heavenly secrets were communicated. But in reality there is much more to her than appears in story books.

The Basic Experience

Jeanne's claim to a special mission was based on her auditions and visions. She heard voices and she saw lights, which she eventually identified primarily as the voices and the figures of the archangel Michael, St. Catherine, and St. Marguerite, and secondarily as a multitude of unnamed angels and, at least once, as the archangel Gabriel. This general summary covers a basic experience and several attempts at the formulation and interpretation of what happened. The basic experience is described very simply:

> When I was in my thirteenth year I heard a voice coming from God to guide me. The first time I was very much afraid. The voice came around noon, in the Summer, in my father's garden; and I had not fasted the day before. I heard a voice from the right, toward the church. And I seldom hear it without light. When I had come to France I often heard the voice. . . . I thought that the voice was a good voice, and I believed that it was sent by God.

[1]See appendix 2.

And after I heard the voice three times I knew it was the voice of an angel. The voice has always guided me well, and I have understood it well.[2]

The fundamental experience is auditive. Jeanne speaks indifferently of "a" voice, "the" voice, and sometimes in the plural, "voices." Had she been more of a theologian she might have preferred the term "word" (in the sense of *parole*, the word spoken, not of *mot*, the grammatical unit). The term she employed simply denoted, on her part, hearing, and it naturally connoted the objective action of a speaker from whom the voice came, to whom it belonged, whose thought and will it expressed. But the experience was at the same time auditory and visual. Light served, as it were, as framework for the sound: "The light comes in front of the voice."[3] And Jeanne insisted: "Seldom have I revelations without light."[4] Even in the castle of Rouen the voices come daily, and "not without light."[5] To the lawyer Jean Beaupère who asked if there had been light when Jeanne "saw the voice and it came to her," she responded: "There was plenty of light from all sides, and this is quite proper. Not all light is for you alone."[6]

For a period of several years, at Domremy, the voice came "twice or thrice a week."[7] When Jeanne came, as she said, to France, she heard it often. Its frequency increased in her prison, where she heard it daily[8] and often several times a day (three times on March 28).[9] While the voice was usually a daylight phenomenon that happened when Jeanne was awake, it also came at night when she was asleep, and then it woke her up.[10] The voice came to her alone, yet also when she was with company and even during the sessions of the hostile tribunal in Rouen, though, in

[2] 2/22: T, 1:47.
[3] 2/24: T, 1:62.
[4] 2/27: T, 1:76.
[5] 3/14: T, 1:147.
[6] 2/27: T, 1:75.
[7] 2/22: T, 1:48.
[8] 3/14: T, 1:147.
[9] 3/28: T, 1:252.
[10] 2/24: T, 1:59.

this case, she "could not understand it well."[11] In her prison Jeanne could at times hardly hear what it said because the guards in her cell made too much noise,[12] as presumably they played cards or dice or some other game to pass the time.

The Voices' Message

At first the voices gave Jeanne spiritual advice and guidance concerning prayer and behavior. The archangel showed her "so many things," she said, "that I firmly believed that it was he."[13] The voice "taught her to behave well and told her to go to church often."[14] Witnesses from Domremy and neighboring villages testified that Jeanne was a simple and pious child, that she made the Sign of the Cross when she heard the church bells ring, that she urged the sexton to ring at the appropriate time (presumably for the Angelus), and that she occasionally encouraged him with a gift of small cakes that she must have baked herself.[15]

At a time that is not specified the voices' message became more precise. They informed Jeanne that "her king would be restored to his kingdom."[16] They also promised "to lead her to Paradise." They called her "Jeanne *la Pucelle,* daughter of God."[17] They spoke of the "misery there was in the kingdom of France."[18] They finally gave her a clear mission: she had to go to France; to free the city of Orléans, which was under siege; and to lead the dauphin to the cathedral of Reims, where he must be properly crowned as king. Jeanne did not receive advance knowledge of the siege, but she knew of it, presumably from public rumor, shortly after it began on October 12, 1428. It was the siege of Orléans that triggered knowledge of her mission. But this mission had a bipolar focus: Orléans and Reims. From that

[11]2/27: T, 1:70.
[12]3/14: Q, 1:153.
[13]3/15: T, 1:163.
[14]2/12: T, 1:48.
[15]Perrin Drapier: Q, 2:413.
[16]T, 1:85.
[17]T, 1:126.
[18]T, 1:163. The French minute says *la pitié,* translated in Latin as *calamitatem.*

moment Jeanne's spiritual way was closely related to the politics of her land and time.

The Coronation

Jeanne had to lead the dauphin to Reims so that he could be made king according to the immemorial tradition of the French monarchy. The king had to be anointed by the archbishop of Reims. Kingship was a quasi-sacrament to which one had access neither by election nor by blood succession but by unction. The coronation and unction of the king were a reenactment of the baptism of Clovis, founder of the monarchy in its Christian dimension, by St. Remi, the archbishop. With or without the Salic law, blood succession designated the proper candidate to the throne, but it was the anointment at Reims that made the king. And this anointment was not with any sort of oil, however holy. It was with the chrism that was preserved in the *sainte ampoule*. It was the unique though probably legendary property of this oil that related the anointed to the baptism of Clovis. For it was believed to have been brought down from heaven by a dove on the occasion of his baptism at Christmas of 497. Clovis (481–511), leader of the Salic Franks, was a pagan, married to a Burgundian princess, St. Clotilde (c. 475–545), who was a Catholic Christian. At Christmas of that year, after a long period of instruction, Clovis espoused the faith of his wife.

The chrism used at the baptism was believed to be preserved in a "holy phial" that was in the custody of the Benedictine monastery of St. Remi, in Reims. The *fleur-de-lys* that became the emblem of the monarchy was no other than a stylized representation of the dove, and its three leaves were taken to designate the theological virtues of faith, hope, and charity. Thus the monarch was seen to be truly anointed by the Lord: his power had a distinctly divine origin, and it was of major importance for the proper order of the kingdom that only a legitimate candidate be anointed with it. The mission of Jeanne *la Pucelle,* daughter of God, who was also in her human lineage daughter of the people, born in the eastern margins of the kingdom through which the Franks had passed as they traveled west after crossing the Rhine, was to ensure the proper transmission of

royal authority at a time when this was threatened by the ambitions of would-be usurpers, the English kings Edward III and
Henry V, by the successful negotiation of the illegitimate treaty
of Troyes, and by the devotion to this ambition of those who
spoke for the child-king Henry VI. In this perspective Jeanne's
mission belonged to the order of the virtue of justice as this
virtue ought to flourish at the highest level of the still-feudal
society of the fifteenth century.

The Siege of Orléans

The immediate purpose of Jeanne's mission was to force
the English opponents of Charles VII to lift the siege of Orléans.
The liberation of Orléans was a necessity if Charles was to receive
the crown, Orléans being the last major city of France that rejected the claims of the English pretender. Were it to fall the
whole valley of the Loire would be open to further invasion. The
dauphin would have to abandon Chinon. Bourges, his chief
commercial town, and Poitiers, his intellectual capital, would
soon be taken by the enemy. Any moderately perceptive strate-
gist could easily see that a three-pronged attack—Burgundian
from the east, English from the north (Paris and Orléans), and
English also from the southwest (their long-time holdings in
Languedoc and Guyenne)—would eliminate all possibility of
large-scale resistance by the Armagnac party. This may well have
been the reason why Robert de Baudricourt had agreed to send
Jeanne to Chinon: she could be a last-resort ally who would delay
what seemed to be the inevitable collapse of the French forces.

Yet there was more to Orléans than a strategic need for action. The fact was that the siege of Orléans was made at the cost
of flouting the most sacred rules of feudal chivalry. It was unciv-
ilized to attack a city when its lord, who was the inhabitants'
providential defender, was himself already a prisoner of the
enemy. The duke of Orléans was another Charles (1391–1465),
the eldest son of Louis (1375–1407) and the Milanese princess
Valentina Visconti (1364–1408). Louis d'Orléans, who was himself the brother of Charles VI of France, had been assassinated in
Paris by men of the duke of Burgundy, Jean *Sans-peur*. Charles
d'Orléans was therefore nephew to Charles VI and first cousin to

the dauphin. Since the disastrous battle of Azincourt (October 24, 1415), however, he was captive in England, where he was kept at first as a prisoner of honor in some of the king's palaces, for the queen was also his cousin. No ransom was set for him for many years.[19] In 1428, when John of Lancaster reluctantly agreed to lay siege to Orléans, the defense of the city was in the able hands of the duke's younger half brother, Jean *le Bâtard,* future comte de Dunois (1403–1468).[20] The chief reason for setting aside the proper code of knightly behavior was simple. The d'Orléans clan provided the strongest support for Charles VII.[21] There was no more effective way to undermine the dauphin than to weaken the power of the duchy of Orléans by taking its central city.[22]

This is the exact point where Jeanne *la Pucelle* enters the fray. To elaborate schemes of military and political power at the expense of justice she opposes the very simplicity of justice. The siege of Orléans is unfair to its lord, unjust to its people, destructive of the proper order of society in the kingdom of France. The campaign in which it fit was, though Jeanne could not have known that, the first of the imperialist wars of modern Europe. At any rate it was shortly after the beginning of the siege of Orléans that the voice assigned Jeanne her unexpected task. Jeanne, however, received no special lights regarding what was going on in Orléans, though she assured her judges that she was given lights as to the duke of Orléans.

[19]McLeod, *Charles,* 204–5.

[20]He was the illegitimate son of Louis d'Orléans and a Dame de Cany.

[21]Charles's first two marriages had reinforced the ties between Orléans and the royal cause. He was married first to his cousin Isabelle, daughter of King Charles VI, in 1406, then to Bonne, daughter of Bernard d'Armagnac, in 1410, and finally to Marie, daughter of the duke of Clèves, in 1440. His first marriage made him brother-in-law to Henry V of England, who was married to his wife's sister, his own cousin Catherine.

[22]In fact, however, it was not the duke of Bedford who insisted on attacking Orléans. It was Thomas Montecute, earl of Salisbury (1388–1428), recently landed in France with a fresh army whose ruthless march from Calais to the Loire river had given him an aura of invincibility. The duke of Bedford, who wished to take Angers first, had reluctantly acquiesced to Salisbury's plan. Wounded at Orléans by a stray cannonball on November 24, 1428, Salisbury died at Meung-sur-Loire on November 27.

Revelation

The result of hearing the voice was what Jeanne called reve-lation, a term that occurs most often in her responses, usually in the form "It was revealed to me . . . ," "My voices told me . . . ," or, in the third person in which her speech was transformed by the secretaries, "She acted by revelation. . . ." The medieval theological language was itself ambiguous in its use of the word *revelatio*. This was not clearly distinguished from *inspiratio* or *suggestio*. Inspirations and suggestions come from the Spirit. What is covered by the word "revelation" is first of all the pub-lic revelation made to the apostles, but also private revelations, communications, insights, intuitions, inspirations. Thomas Aquinas indeed taught that knowledge of the articles of faith comes from "divine revelation," which necessarily is from above. But he also held that in the normal way of divine Providence the revelation is communicated to ordinary people by the teachers of the faith, just as it reaches the lower angels by way of the higher ones in the angelic hierarchies described by Denys the Are-opagite.[23] By the same token revelations can be made by angels to men and women, and then of course to a young girl in a small village. At this level, revelation becomes indistinguishable from the sudden inspiration anyone may feel to act in a certain way.

Given the ambiguity of the theological language then used in regard to inspiration and revelation, it is understandable that the vernacular, especially when spoken by the illiterate, should be looser still. Jeanne's revelations were insights, certitudes that came to her through voices or that she attributed to voices. But to her they meant absolute certainty. She saw the angels, she said, as clearly as she saw her judges. She knew that she would free Or-léans as certainly as she believed in God.

From what Jeanne said, the revelations given by her voices concerned chiefly herself, her mission, the king, the duke Charles d'Orléans, and a few other persons. She was enlightened about Catherine de la Rochelle and her false claims to have visions of a white lady. In this case, however, Jeanne was also able to reach a negative judgment. Feeling suspicious, Jeanne volunteered to

[23] *Summa theologiae* I-II, q. 2, art. 6.

spend the night with Catherine. As Jeanne had slept part of the night, Catherine assured her that the white lady had indeed come and that she had not been able to wake her up. For the second night, however, Jeanne had taken enough rest during the day to be able to stay awake all night. And the white lady never appeared. Catherine de la Rochelle was a fake. Jeanne advised her "to go back to her husband, look after her house, and feed her children."[24]

Jeanne also received lights concerning the bishop of Beauvais. What these were she did not specify, but she gave him due warning that he should be careful to judge justly, for otherwise he would be in grave danger. She agreed to recite *Pater noster* and *Ave Maria* if the bishop heard her confession, which he refused. Instead he made the offer that one or two other persons hear her say the two prayers; but she refused again unless they heard her confession. Her point was evidently that the sacrament of penance would place the confessor—priest or bishop—in a different position. Canonically, what the priest would then know at the internal forum could not be used at the external forum, and he would be caught in a dilemma between the internal and the external. This was a neat maneuver. But the bishop of Beauvais could easily see through it, and of course he would not place himself or some other judges in that awkward position.[25]

At another level Jeanne disclaimed any information regarding the poor health of the duke of Lorraine. With her usual frankness she advised him to lead a better life and to dismiss his mistress. Likewise, she had no information regarding the identity of the true pope. Jeanne's basic experience is thus strictly focused on awareness of her mission. Yet few details, if any, were given her on the situation in Orléans.[26] The voice did not cover extraneous

[24]T, 1:79.

[25]Yet one of the assessors had no such scruples. Nicolas Loyseleur lied to her when he disguised himself as a man from Lorraine, a friend; he visited her before many of the court sessions and advised her not to trust the lawyers; when he revealed that he was a priest, he heard Jeanne's confession several times and was the only one allowed to do so by Bishop Cauchon: Q, 3:136, 141.

[26]The day before the first Sunday in Lent an English column bringing smoked herrings to the English side was ineffectively intercepted by French

points. Even though she at times expressed the hope to liberate the duke of Orléans and even the Holy Sepulcher in Jerusalem, this was not part of her mission. When she spoke in that way, as Dunois reported, it was by way of conversation and jokingly.[27] In her serious mood she spoke only of liberating Orléans and leading the dauphin to Reims. As she assured Peter Manuel, she did not know precisely when she would be captured.[28] Yet Jeanne was not taken in when Jean de Luxembourg, the Burgundian vassal who had held her captive and had sold her to John of Lancaster, visited her in Rouen and spoke of putting her up for ransom if only she would promise not to fight anymore against their party. "In God's name," she replied, "you mock me, for I know well that you have neither the will nor the power to do so." And as he insisted she added: "I know well that these English will make me die, believing that after my death they will obtain the kingdom of France; but if they were a hundred thousand more *godons* they will not have the kingdom."[29]

The Meaning of Virginity

There was a deeper dimension to Jeanne's experience than learning about her mission. This deeper dimension emerges from

---

raiders, who were badly mauled in the encounter. The evidence is too weak to argue that Jeanne informed Robert de Baudricourt of this event on the very day it took place. The statement that she did is found in some of the fifteenth-century chronicles: "Journal du siège" (Q, 4:125), "Chronique de la Pucelle" (Q, 4:206).

[27]Dunois: Q, 3:16.

[28]Manuel: Q, 3:200.

[29]Haimond de Macy: Q, 3:121–22. Macy reports that the earl of Stafford drew his dagger but his angry gesture was stopped by the earl of Warwick, who as governor of the castle had the responsibility of keeping Jeanne alive until she was burned. *Godon*, a deformation of *goddamn*, was a nickname given by the French to the English for obvious reasons. Compare Jeanne's statement with her prediction of English defeat: "I say that before seven years the English will lose a more important piece than before Orléans, and they will lose all of France" (3/1: T, 1:83). This was said in 1430; Charles VII regained Paris in 1437, seven years later; then Rouen in 1450; Bordeaux and Bayonne in 1451. Only Calais, conquered in 1347 by Edward III, remained in English hands; it fell to François de Guise under Queen Mary in 1558.

her confession that the first time she heard the voice "she took the vow of virginity for as long as it would please God."[30] This is all the more significant as Jeanne also admitted that, this first time, she was very much afraid and that she did not yet understand that an angel had spoken to her. At that moment the vow of virginity was not the outcome of a deliberation. It was not a well-reasoned choice but a spontaneous action that Jeanne found herself taking. And she took it because in the depths of her being she was transformed by the encounter. Despite her original fear she suddenly acquired a whole new purpose in life, a purpose that could not be better pursued than through an exclusive commitment to God. In the context of her time and place this self-giving to God was spontaneously put in the form of vowed virginity.

Jeanne never presumed of her own strength. She did not take perpetual vows. What she did was much more radical. She placed herself and her future entirely in the hands of God: virginity "as long as it would please God." And virginity as she understood it was not merely a matter of sexual continence. It was a spiritual attitude: "I must keep the vow and promise that I have made to Our Lord, to keep well my virginity of body and of soul."[31] What is virginity of soul? Jeanne was quite clear about it: "One cannot clean one's conscience too much."[32] She cleaned her conscience through the ordinary means of the Church, the sacraments, and primarily the sacrament of penance. There were periods in her campaign when, according to her chaplain Jean Pasquerel, she came to confession nearly every day.[33] She also received Communion more often than was the general custom. But the heart of her virginity of soul was an utter reliance on God and God's gracious will, not on herself and her own actions.

The transformation of the self that Jeanne underwent the first time she heard the voice reorganized her life around virginity of soul. And this was possible because it first of all refocused her very self on her virgin soul. In the process she became *la*

[30]2/27, T, 1:76–7.
[31]T, 1:123.
[32]T, 1:150.
[33]Pasquerel: Q, 3:104.

Pucelle while never ceasing to be Jeannette or Jeanne. The result of her transformation was not a narcissistic self-absorption. It was a gift of self to the service of justice. She had to fight for justice if she wished to keep her virgin soul.

The Doctrine of St. John of the Cross

The central spiritual experience of Jeanne *la Pucelle* should be understood as being strictly mystical in the traditional sense of this word in the Church's spiritual tradition. Jeanne was moved by the Spirit when she vowed to keep her virginity as an expression of her virgin soul and when she went on to fulfill her mission in the defense of what she identified as the proper order of justice. This may be illustrated with the help of St. John of the Cross' explanation of visions and auditions in *The Ascent of Mount Carmel:*

> Through these senses spiritual persons can, and usually do, perceive supernatural representations and objects.
>
> As for sight, they are wont to have visions of images and persons from the other life: of saints, of images of the good and bad angels; and of some unusual sights and splendors.
>
> Through hearing they apprehend certain extraordinary words, sometimes from the vision, and at other times without seeing the one who speaks.[34]

It is the teaching of the Spanish mystic that supernatural information regarding particulars ought to be ignored even if it certainly comes from God. Thus a profound asceticism affects not only all reliance on external means of devotion but, much more profoundly, all use of extraordinary means. For the basic principle of the spiritual life is faith: "Faith is the only proximate means of union with God."[35] The knowledge that is given in faith is never of individualities and particularities, for neither God nor any of the three divine Persons or any one of the innumer-

---

[34] *The Ascent of Mount Carmel,* bk. 2, ch. 11, n. 1 (Kieran Kavanaugh and Otilio Rodriguez, *The Collected Works of St. John of the Cross* (Washington, D.C.: ICM Publications, 1991) 179. The text continues with spiritual sense, taste, and touch.

[35] John of the Cross, *Ascent,* bk. 2, ch. 9.

able divine attributes is a particular entity that could be connumerated with other particular entities.

Jeanne, as she said, saw angelic personages and heard them speak; she touched two saints and smelled their perfume. Yet her attitude when she saw, heard, smelled, and touched was quite different from the one that, approximately a century and a half later, John of the Cross would recommend: "Such representations and feelings . . . must always be rejected. Even though some may be from God, this rejection is no affront to him. Nor will one, by rejecting and not wanting them, fail to receive the effect and fruit God wishes to produce through them."[36] Jeanne, of course, was not a theologian or a reader of spiritual literature. She could hardly have been acquainted, even from hearsay, with the numerous medieval mystics who preceded her. Never in her career, in Domremy or later, did she even confide in or trust a spiritual adviser or a director of conscience. She revealed nothing to the pastor of Domremy or to any other priest or preacher. She went to confession frequently, but this was for absolution and the sacramental grace, for cleaning her soul, not for advice regarding what she knew as coming to her from God through angelic voices.

Admittedly, medieval spiritual writers generally did not anticipate the radical negations that became part of the spirituality of the reformed Carmel in the wake of St. John of the Cross. Rather, they tended to highlight the spiritual powers that God's grace is able to enkindle in the soul. They commonly favored the contemplation of pictures, real or imaginary, the telling and hearing of pious legends vaguely modeled on the Scriptures, the paraliturgical shows of edifying theater, the exploitation of visual symbols, the drawing of maps of the spiritual journey, the movements of processions and pilgrimages as models of what St. Bonaventure called "the itinerary of the soul into God." Jeanne's mother, faithful to her name, went on pilgrimage soon after Jeanne left for Chinon. She traveled far to pray to the black Virgin, Notre-Dame du Puy, in the hilly country of south-central France some four hundred kilometers in a straight line south-southwest of Domremy, two hundred kilometers from Poitiers where her

---

[36]John of the Cross, *Ascent,* bk. 2, ch. 9., n. 5, p. 181.

daughter was at the time. The Augustinian friar Jean Pasquerel testified that he had met Jeanne's mother with some of her soldier companions at Le Puy, and they had persuaded him to seek for her.[37]

Elementary though it was, Jeanne's formation had certainly made her familiar with the images of angels and saints that in statuary, painting, and church glass represented the heavenly kingdom and that pilgrims visited in their many shrines. The world of everyday chores was filled with tokens that could easily lead her thoughts to God and the blessed inhabitants of heaven.

The ensuing religious mentality that surrounded Jeanne was all too prone to take the sign for the reality, to value the marvelous and the extraordinary instead of divine grace's silent conversion of the heart. Jeanne, however, escaped that pitfall. Her spiritual focus was never on supernatural happenings, in which she could easily have taken pride. What happened in her soul is best explained by John of the Cross. When she was very much afraid and took the vow of virginity for as long as it would please God, it is clear that Jeanne experienced what the reformer of Carmel would call a "substantial word."[38] Indeed, she frequently heard what the Mystical Doctor would call "successive words," and "formal words," the former sounding outside and heard through the ears, the latter formulated within, in mind and imagination. Yet Jeanne was never attached to them. John of the Cross, precisely, declares that they ought to be ignored. "Substantial words" are of another kind. They cannot be ignored or rejected. They are not subject to deliberate acceptance. Whether formulated in words or not, they are creative acts that occur when God does what they signify.

When the voice first came to Jeanne she found herself in one instant substantially changed. In her spiritual substance she became a virgin soul, justified and purified by God. In her self-understanding she was nothing other than an offering to the will of God; she was *la Pucelle,* a little girl who holds herself to be of no value, a virgin of no importance in her own eyes, satisfied with

[37]Pasquerel: Q, 3:101.
[38]John of the Cross, *Ascent,* bk. 2, chs. 28 and 31, pp. 255, 263–64.

simply being what God would make her, the clay that God would shape, the garden God would till. As she declared, "My words and my doings are all in the hands of God."[39] And again: "I know for certain that Our Lord has always been master of my actions and that the Enemy [the devil] has never had any power over me."[40]

Jeanne's mission was to be a virgin soul. Only a virgin soul can engage in the struggle for justice without feeling hatred for the unjust, can obtain victory without taking pride in success, can be the innocent victim of a political and ecclesiastical machine bent on destroying her without acrimony toward those who have engineered her condemnation, can face the threat of torture with equanimity, and can go to death by fire with full confidence in God. When she was in the torture chamber Jeanne simply declared: "I have asked my voices if I would be burnt; they answered that I should rely on Our Lord and he will assist me."[41]

[39]T, 1:158.
[40]T, 1:349.
[41]T, 1:349-350.

FOUR

Jeanne's Angels

At a time that cannot be ascertained exactly, Jeanne began to identify the voices that spoke to her. This happened, as she stated, after she heard the voice three times. She also said that she had seen him "several times before she knew that it was St. Michael."[1] When questioned as to what made her recognize the archangel, she said that it was "by the speech and language of angels." Jeanne was not thinking of unknown tongues in the modern pentecostal sense of the terms. Rather, she meant that what the voice taught her was good and appropriate to angels. The archangel "taught her and showed her so many things that she firmly believed it was he."[2] He told her "to be a good child, and that God would help her" and also "to behave well, to go to church often."[3]

The archangel did not always come alone. He was sometimes accompanied by other angels,[4] though Jeanne does not claim to have always seen them. On May 9 in the torture chamber Jeanne was shown various instruments that could be applied to her body to force her to speak. Faced with this frightening prospect she reacted with both defiance and confidence. On the one hand, she protested that torture could not make her say more than she had already said, and in any case if she were forced to speak she would later declare that it had been extorted from her. On the other hand, the fear of torture was dwarfed by the remembrance that the archangel Gabriel had comforted her "at

[1] T, 1:162.
[2] T, 1:163.
[3] T, 1:48.
[4] T, 1:73.

the last Holy Cross."[5] This was said on May 15; the last Holy Cross was the feast of the Invention of the Holy Cross, on May 3.[6] Jeanne knew it was Gabriel because her voices told her so. The archangel, whose name expresses the greatness and nobility of God,[7] appeared appropriately at a time when Jeanne, impeded from going to church, was commemorating the Cross of Jesus in her heart. In the name of the feast, "invention" means discovery, and Jeanne was about to discover the awesome weight of her own cross. Soon, however, in the communications between the heavenly world and herself, the saints Catherine and Marguerite became her most frequent visitors. Their coming had been announced by the archangel Michael.[8]

The Patron of the Monarchy

The question naturally comes to mind, why did Jeanne see and hear Michael? Why Catherine and Marguerite rather than, for instance, her own patron saint? Why did she never see the Virgin Mary, Mother of God?

Michael, the leader of the heavenly armies against Lucifer, was an important political figure connected with the monarchy of the Franks since the baptism of Clovis. It was popularly believed that Clovis was assisted by the archangel in his victory at Tolbiac in 496 against the Alamans after he promised to adopt the Catholic religion of his wife. The great emperor Charlemagne had himself been devoted to both Michael and Gabriel, the latter being seen as a special protector of the Carolingian dynasty. Both the Germanic and the French peoples, who had equally inherited the tradition of Charlemagne, identified Michael as the heavenly patron of their respective nations. St. Boniface (ca. 675–754/55), the apostle of Germany, is credited with the consecration of the German lands to the first of the archangels.

---

[5]T, 1:349.

[6]This feast was first celebrated in the Gallican liturgy of the eighth century. It was suppressed in 1960 by John XXIII.

[7]Gabriel means "*El* (God) is powerful."

[8]T, 1:162.

At the time of Jeanne Darc the abbey and fortress of Mont-St.-Michel, off the coast of Normandy, remained loyal to Charles VII, and during the entire Hundred Years' War it successfully repelled all the English attempts to storm it in spite of its isolated location far from the Armagnacs' Continental strongholds. The situation of Vaucouleurs was somewhat similar to that of Mont-St.-Michel.[9] Its immediate neighbor to the west, the county of Champagne, was of the Burgundian party. Its neighbors to the north and east, the duchies of Bar and Lorraine, were also inclined for reasons of geography to favor the Burgundians. This may have prompted more devotion to St. Michael in the upper valley of the Meuse.

After the fall of Paris to the English in 1419 the dauphin had had his flags painted with a picture of the archangel Michael. It was the picture of St. Denys, founder and first bishop of the diocese of Paris, believed to be the disciple of St. Paul converted at the Areopagus (Acts 17:33), which had hitherto adorned the royal pennon. But the abbey of St. Denys, just north of Paris, was now in English hands. Wherever St. Denys had been represented on the standards of France, the dauphin had ordered the archangel Michael painted. To fight for the dauphin meant to fight alongside of Michael the archangel. This complex of images around the archangel's name could only be enriched by the local devotion to Michael the archangel that already flourished in the Meuse valley. Michael was the patron saint of the duchy of Bar. The influential abbey of St. Mihiel, founded in 709 some fifty-three kilometers north of Domremy, bore a local form of his name. There was a pilgrimage to St. Michael in the vicinity of the city of Toul. And in the dioceses of Metz, Toul, and Verdun forty-six churches were dedicated to him.[10]

[9]Tournai was another city in a similar situation. Having opted for Charles VII in 1426, it was never conquered by the enemy; on June 25, 1429, Jeanne invited the city to send a delegation to the coronation in Reims (Q, 5:123–25). Tournai is now in Belgium.

[10]As stated in T, 2:72, note 2.

Angelic Light

Jeanne's description of the archangel and of the angels who often accompanied him remained general, even vague. This may well have been intentional, for it is obvious from the minutes of her trial that her judges and those among their assistants who interrogated her were attempting to confuse her and thus lead her into contradictions or unacceptable statements. They switched from one kind of question to another without warning. They followed no logical or chronological order. Jeanne was smart enough to see this, and she retaliated in kind. Yet her answers had to remain within narrow parameters, since she refused to betray what she considered secrets, and she was determined to avoid helping the enemy in the ongoing struggle for the kingship of France. Within these bounds she tried to embarrass the judges by her answers, or to leave them in the dark, and occasionally to laugh at them and point out the absurdity of the questions.

As Jeanne describes them, the angels and saints are always accompanied by light when they communicate with her. That the heavenly world knows no night was a commonplace of medieval angelology. Under the influence of Johannes Scotus Eriugena (810–877), who had translated the works of Denys in Latin, the Dionysian theory of hierarchic illuminations had entered Western theology: The higher angels illumine the lower ones. If illumination is understood as a kind of teaching, it is parallel to the process of human knowing, as when the learned teach the ignorant. Thomas Aquinas himself regarded the angelic illuminations as the model for the transmission of human knowledge:

> The explanation of the articles of faith comes from divine revelation, for the articles of faith are beyond natural reason. But the divine revelation is by a certain order and reaches the lower through the higher, like men through angels, and lower angels through higher angels. Therefore likewise it is proper that the explanation of faith reach the lower humans through the higher. And therefore, as the higher angels, who rule the lower ones, have a fuller knowledge of divine realities,[11] so the higher humans, to whom

[11]This principle comes from Dionysius the Areopagite (Denys, Pseudo-Denys) in his *Caelestis Hierarchia,* ch. 1.

teaching pertains, must have a fuller knowledge of the articles of faith and must believe them more explicitly.[12]

The Dionysian description of the angelic illuminations completed the theory, derived from Augustine, that human knowing is the fruit of a divine illumination of the mind. That not only the Word of God but also angels could illumine human intellects was generally accepted, in keeping with the theology of Denys. Thus the Scholastic theologians were led to reflect deeply, especially in the Franciscan school of St. Bonaventure, on the nature and function of light. John Duns Scotus was an exception in that he denied that angels or devils are able to affect the mind directly. But as he could not deny all stories of angelic visions, he moved the locus of their apparitions from within the soul to the outside world, where angels assume a bodily shape and are heard speaking a human language.[13]

In any case, intellectual light being placed at the center of human experience, it is not surprising that metaphors of light should have spread to all branches of study. Such metaphors had an impact on biblical exegesis, as when Peter Comestor in his widely read *Historia scholastica* explained the *Fiat lux* of Gen 1:3 ("Let there be light") as marking the division between the angels of light faithful to God and those among the angelic creatures who opted to become angels of darkness. The angels of light participate in the light of the divine Word. The angels of darkness, the devils, try, though in vain, to obscure it.

Such imaging of the angelic world was common. It developed with special flourish in commentaries on the Apocalypse of John, in the miniatures, also called "illuminations" (in French, *enluminures,* from Latin *in* and *lumen*), that enhanced these commentaries and other biblical writings. The angelic world was prominent in Dante's *Paradiso* (finalized in 1321): Dante is led by the Latin poet Virgil through inferno and purgatory, and by his idealized young lady Beatrice through paradise. But he evidently encounters angels. And the angelic nature is explained to

[12] *Summa theologiae*, I–II, q. 2, a. 6.
[13] Georges Tavard, *Die Engel (Handbuch der Dogmengechischte)* (Freiburg: Herder, 1968) 2b, 2:74–5.

him as being created light, a light that, like a prism, reflects the one Light of God in myriads of mirrors:

> The angelic nature mounts in number so
> Past measure that no speech was ever skilled
> Nor mortal thought, to cast for a throw; . . .
> The primal light whose beams irradiate
> This nature, is absorbed through avenues
> Many as the splendors whereto it is mate; . . .
> That sweetness grows within them fiery-bright
> Or warm according to the mode they use.
> See now the Eternal Virtue's breadth and height,
> Since it has made itself so vast a store
> Of mirrors upon which to break its light,
> Remaining in itself one, as before.[14]

Statues and Paintings

Jeanne, of course, knew no more of such theories and descriptions than the little that could transpire through popular preaching. Yet her own world, the common world of the peasantry, was no less filled with images of light. When she affirmed that her voices were always accompanied by light, even if this light was unperceived, she described what was commonly painted on the walls of churches. The inside of most medieval churches were decorated with scenes taken from the Old and the New Testaments, from early apocryphal stories, and from the lives of the saints. Jeanne had certainly not seen beautiful Gothic cathedrals in her childhood, for there were none in her immediate area. But this does not mean that she did not look at the paintings in the ordinary churches and chapels she knew: the village churches of Domremy, Greux, Maxey; the churches of Neufchâteau, which were not much larger; small chapels like that of Notre-Dame de Bermont hidden in the woods some two kilometers north of Domremy, the site of a hermitage where Jeanne frequently went to pray by herself. When she went to Toul in the matter of her alleged promise of marriage, and on the way to visit

---

[14]Canto 29, lines 136–45, trans. Laurence Binyon, *The Portable Dante,* rev. ed. (New York: Viking Press, 1976) 522.

the duke of Lorraine in Nancy, she must have seen something of the yet unfinished cathedral.[15] Near Nancy, as we have mentioned, she visited the old shrine of St.-Nicolas-de-Port,[16] which housed a relic of the famed saint Nicholas of Myre. In Nancy itself it is likely that she prayed in the large chapel of the duke's palace and in the nearby church of St. George.[17] It is safe to assume that all these churches and chapels were decorated, if not always in the most skilled fashion.

The popular imaging of angels echoed the theological notion that the angels are themselves created reflections of the divine Word, who himself is, as stated in the Creed, *Lumen de Lumine,* divine Light from divine Light. In Jeanne's life the voice is a channel of the Word, and the light a channel of the Light. Both voice and light sent her back to Christ as the original Word and Light of God. Thus the familiarity with angels and saints apparent in her life was profoundly christocentric. It is Christ who is her Lord as well as the Lord of the angels and the saints in "the kingdom of Paradise." As these inhabitants of heaven are entirely at the service of God, so Jeanne desires to be totally given to God, happen what may to her body here below. This is the central line of her spirituality. Jeanne expressed it in a lapidary formula: "Our Lord the first served."[18]

[15]According to Marina Warner, Jeanne saw the cathedral of Toul "from a great distance" when walking "southward from Domremy." In fact, Toul is north of Domremy! She adds that "the sight, so striking today, must have been equally unforgettable then" (*Joan of Arc,* 93). In reality, the cathedral was still under construction, the tall towers being erected later in the century.

[16]The present Gothic basilica was built in the sixteenth century, but there was a previous church on the spot.

[17]The ducal chapel still stands, next to the dukes' Gothic palace. St. George's church was destroyed in the eighteenth century to make room for an extension of the dukes' palace in the new classical style. This is now called *le palais du gouvernement.*

[18]*Notre Sire premier servi,* Latinized as *Deo primitus servito* (3/31: T, 1:288).

Visions of Angels

When Jeanne reported that the king also had "several apparitions and fine revelations" she was naturally pressed for details. But she refused to say anything more, for she never considered herself authorized to betray the king's secrets: "I will not tell you yet; but go to the king, he will tell you."[19] As to what she saw of Michael and the angels, her responses could be shifty. Here again, the true mystics are reluctant to speak of their experiences. Jeanne declared, "I believe that I am not telling you plainly what I know."[20] Indeed, she insisted on the reality of her experience: "I saw them with my bodily eyes, as well as I see you. When they left me I cried, and I would have wished that they take me with them."[21] Yet at times she refused to answer. Taking refuge behind her counsel, she protested, "I am not permitted to tell you."

> *Question:* Does the voice have sight?[22] eyes?
> *Answer:* I will not tell you; it is said among little children that sometimes people are hanged for telling the truth.[23]

This answer is particularly significant. Jeanne sensed that in spite of their repeated affirmations of solicitude toward her, the interrogators were only trying to send her to the scaffold. They were looking for signs of magic in her life. Their minds were focused on the Fairies' Tree,[24] on the slope down from the oaks' forest, a few hundred yards south of Domremy; on the nearby springs, *la fontaine des Fées* (the Fairies' Spring), also known as *des Fiévreux* (of the Feverish), near the Tree, and *la fontaine des*

[19]2/22: T, 1:52.
[20]T, 1:60.
[21]T, 1:74.
[22]*La voix, Jeanne, est-ce qu'elle a un regard?*
[23]2/24: T, 1:62. When asked what she meant by this, Jeanne did not answer (3/17: T, 1:164).
[24]The Fairies' Tree, *l'arbre des fées*. The legend of the Fairies' Tree must have originated in a pun. There was a *fay*, or *fayard* (beechtree, *hêtre* in modern French). But *fay* (from the Latin *fagus*) and *fée* (from *fata*) have the same sound, whence the popular deformation into a fairies' tree. *Bois chenu* ("white wood" or "old wood") was itself a deformation of *bois chesnu* (from *chesne* or *chêne*, oak).

Groseillers (the Currant Bushes' Spring); on whether their waters had healing powers, on why children gathered and girls danced around the tree, on the making and hanging of wreaths and garlands, on the mandrake that Jeanne allegedly wore (which she denied), on whether she kissed the rings she wore on her fingers.

Jeanne's Assurance

The judges' repeated but futile attempts to find obsolete pagan practices in the local folklore of Domremy could only mean that they were sniffing for sorcery. Yet witchcraft was not a major concern of the clergy in the first half of the fifteenth century. At the most it was a possible token of heresy. And it was heresy that the judges were after, for only obdurate heresy manifested by relapsing into it after renouncing it could legally send heretics to the pyre. Whatever Jeanne said in plain language could be turned against her by lawyers who were skilled at playing with words and who could pretend to find hidden meanings where none was intended. How could she tell a good angel from an evil one, the interrogator asked on March 15, "if the enemy took the form or sign of an angel?"[25] Angels of darkness can be mistaken for angels of light. Alleged visions may be delusions. Since the accused is unlearned, how can she know which is which? Jeanne's answers to this type of question was simple and straight: She certainly would know "if it is St. Michael or a counterfeit that looks like him." This of course could never satisfy a tribunal bound to find her guilty of obdurate heresy so that she could be handed over to the secular arm of the king of England and be burned.

After the liberation of Orléans while she was in the castle of Loches with the dauphin, Jeanne was asked by the king's confessor, Christophe d'Harcourt, bishop of Castres, if she would not tell the king how her counsel spoke to her. According to Dunois "she blushed as she answered: I well imagine what you wish to know, and I will tell you willingly." She then reported that when she feels that no one believes what she says in the name of God

[25]T, 1:162.

she retires by herself and complains about it before God. Her prayer done, she hears a voice: "Daughter of God, go, go, go, I will assist you, go!" Dunois continues:

> When she heard this voice she was in joy and wished to remain always in that state; and, what is still more, as she repeated the words of her voices she was in an extraordinary ecstasy and lifted her eyes to heaven.[26]

On Tuesday, March 1, Jeanne's unnamed interrogator asked about St. Michael's aspect when he appeared. No, she did not see a crown and she knew nothing of his clothes. Asked if he was naked, she made fun of the question: "Do you think Our Lord cannot afford to clothe him?"[27] Likewise about his hair: "Why should they have been clipped? . . . No, I do not know if he had hair." She volunteered the information that she had not seen the archangel since she left the castle of Crotoy and that she does not see him very often. The interrogator asked if the archangel had his scale with him. Jeanne responded: "I do not know. When I see him I have great joy; it seems to me that when I see him that I am not in mortal sin."[28]

It seems clear from these responses that when Jeanne says that she sees the archangel she does not mean that she perceives the details of his appearance. Rather, she senses his presence with certainty. The archangel is with her. She cannot tell if he has a crown on his head; she does not know about his hair or about his clothes. In other words, what she sees does not come through her eyes. Nor is it only an interior impression or a psychological conviction. It fits in the category of the spiritual senses by which one can have an experiential knowledge of the divine realities, in a perspective that was developed by Origen.[29] However vivid they can be, the bodily senses are weak intimations of the spiritual senses, through which the faithful soul is in-

---

[26]Q, 3:12.

[27]T, 1, 87.

[28]A passage like this is obviously not compatible with the bizarre idea that angels would be a metaphorical term evoking bishops with floating capes.

[29]Jean Daniélou, *Origène* (Paris: La Table Ronde, 1948) 298–301.

troduced to the intimacy of her heavenly Spouse. Through a higher form of hearing Jeanne heard the voice, not of the Spouse in person but of the Spouse's envoy, the first of the archangels. Through a higher form of sight she has perceived his spiritual presence. Through a higher form of touch she has been touched by some of the angels and saints who have visited her, and she in turn has touched them. Through a higher form of smell she has sensed their spiritual perfume. The only sense that Jeanne does not mention is taste. Yet she longed after it when she begged to be allowed to attend Mass and to receive her Lord in the Eucharist.

Again, on March 17, Jeanne explained that Michael "has the bearing of a true good man."[30] But she will say no more about "his clothing and the rest." Yet she is absolutely certain that what she sees is the archangel Michael. For she adds: "As to the angels, I have seen them with my own eyes, and you will draw nothing more from me. I believe the words and deeds of St. Michael who appeared to me, as firmly as I believe that Our Lord suffered his death and passion for us." The reason for this "is the good advice, comfort, and devotion that he has entrusted and given to me."

Questions of Angelology

According to an early Christian tradition inherited from late Judaism angels are the original inhabitants of heaven, created before the material universe. They form the court of the heavenly king. Many of them also move about the world on divine errands. Jeanne had no reason to question what her mother and the parish priest of Domremy must have said about them. She could not doubt that angels care about God's other creatures. On March 13 she declared that angels often come among Christians and are not seen, but she has seen them many times among Christians.[31] Yet in her prison the archangel does not appear. Since Jeanne has not seen him since Le Crotoy, she has been deprived of his presence for over one month.

[30]T, 1:165.
[31]T, 1:125.

The topic of angels and visions of angels offered the tribunal fertile ground for embarrassing questions. Asking Jeanne about the scale was meant to confuse her. In the Christian tradition the archangel Michael belongs to the highest group of spiritual creatures, much higher than the "psycho-pomp" angels who weigh the souls and their merits. But such distinctions, like the more elaborate heavenly hierarchies of Denys that were universally accepted in medieval angelology, may have been lost in popular art. In any case, if there was a trap in the question about the scales Jeanne did not fall into it, for she drew attention to the spiritual meaning of the angelic presence: The archangel would not come if she were in mortal sin. And as the questioner turns to sin and confession she again avoids the new pitfall he tries to open before her: "She responded that she did not know if she has been in mortal sin and she does not think she has done the works of it. And may it not please God, she said, that I ever be in mortal sin or that I do or did its works, of which my soul would be charged."[32]

More annoying for Jeanne could have been the question about the creation of angels that she confronted on March 3. What triggered the question was Jeanne's assertion that she has indeed seen Michael and Gabriel with her own eyes and that she believes that they exist as firmly as she believes that God exists:[33]

> Asked if she believes that God formed them in those heads in which she has seen them, she answers: Yes.

> Asked if she believes that it is in this form and manner that God created them at the beginning, she answers: You will hear no more for the time being except what I have answered.

In other words, while she believed that the angelic heads she had seen were made by God, Jeanne would not presume to know in what form God created the angels. She was led to the brink of what could have been seen as a claim to know more than the

[32]T, 1:87.
[33]T, 1:92–3. Similarly, on March 17 Jeanne declared that she "as firmly believes the words and acts of St. Michael who appeared to her as she believes that Our Lord Jesus Christ suffered his death and passion for us" (165). Jeanne emphasized the reality, not the mode, of the experience.

Church about the creation of angels. But she remained firmly anchored in the sobriety that is a mark of her faith.

The Angel and the Crown

On March 13 Jeanne told the judges a story that has puzzled most of her biographers. As she was asked about the nature of the sign by which she persuaded the dauphin of the authenticity of her call and mission, she began by evading the question. Earlier, on the first day of March, she had simply refused to answer, stating that she could not reveal the sign without perjury. Then, on March 13, she affirmed that it was an angel who brought the king a sign.[34] She heard later that "more than three hundred persons saw the sign." She explained: "The sign was that the angel guaranteed to the king, by bringing him the crown, that he would have the entire kingdom of France, with God's help and through her own work." This took place at the castle of Chinon in the first few days of Jeanne's arrival.

Pressed for details by Jean Le Maistre, the vice-inquisitor who had been most reluctant to take part in the trial, she said that this happened around midday some time in April or March. In March this would have been the sign she gave the dauphin the first time they met in Chinon, when they talked privately and what she said to him out of hearing seemed to lift a burden from his soul. But we know from testimonies in the nullity investigation that in Jeanne's first audience with the king there was no presentation of a crown. In April this would have been after the approval of Jeanne's mission by the scholars in Poitiers, shortly before the march on Orléans.

Simon Charles held a responsible position at the court. As *maître des requêtes* he had to sort out the petitions of all kinds that came to the king.[35] As he reported them, the proceedings in Chinon were quite simple. Jeanne was admitted to the king's presence on the advice of his counsel and of several churchmen who had already talked to her. She spoke with the king for a long

[34]T, 1:133–34.
[35]By the time of the nullity inquiry he had become *président de la cour des comptes,* in charge of keeping track of the king's income and expenses.

time out of hearing. He seemed pleased. But he acted with caution, sending her first to Poitiers to be examined by several ecclesiastics and doctors of the Sorbonne.[36] One of the Poitiers examiners, the Dominican Seguin Seguin, told Jeanne that they could not simply take her word for it and then advise the king to give her soldiers whose life would then be endangered. If God wants them to believe the story of her call, there should be some sign that they ought to do so. Jeanne retorted: "In God's name, I have not come to Poitiers to show signs; but take me to Orléans and I will show you the signs for which I have been sent."[37] After some three weeks of interrogations and debates the churchmen's report was favorable to the authenticity of her mission. But their decision was based on no other signs than Jeanne's answers to their questions. In Poitiers the context had been friendly. In Rouen it was hostile. This made an enormous difference. Yet in either case the crown was the anticipated sign of the crowning, and the crowning was the ultimate sign that Jeanne's mission was authentic.

When asked about the sign by the hostile judges Jeanne described it through a symbolic tale. Yes, she brought a crown to the king from her temporary lodgings in the house of Guillaume Bellier.[38] The crown, she said, was of gold. It was from God, and no mere craftsman could have made one like it. "And it was in the form of a crown."[39] An angel brought it when Jeanne was in

[36]Q, 3:203. Some of these scholars were listed by the king's counselor, François Garivel (Q, 3:19): a former professor of theology, Pierre de Versailles, then abbot of Talmont, later bishop of Digne and then of Meaux; the Dominicans Pierre Lambert and Guillaume Alveri; the Carmelite Pierre Seguin, all doctors in Holy Scripture; Mathieu Lesage and Guillaume Lemarié, bachelors in theology. There was also the Dominican Seguin Seguin, who himself testified and named some of the theologians: Jean Lombart, Guillaume Lemaire, Guillaume Aymeri, Pierre Turrelure, Jacques Madelon (Q, 3:203).

[37]Q, 3:205.

[38]The name is given by Raoul de Gaucourt, who adds that "his wife was a woman of great devotion and most excellent reputation: *femina magnae devotionis et commendatissimae famae*" (Q, 3:17).

[39]3/13: T, 1:140. This is said in answer to a question about the smell of the crown: *Elle sent bon et sentira; mais qu'elle soit bien gardée ainsi qu'il appartient. Et était en manière de couronne.*

prayer in the house. Both of them went to the palace and entered into the king's presence. The angel went in first and Jeanne followed, but it was Jeanne who said, "Sir, this is your sign; take it." There were also many other angels, but the courtiers who were present did not generally see them. Several of the bystanders saw the chief angel; others saw the crown but not the angel. Among the angels who were present several had wings, others not. St. Catherine and St. Marguerite were there too. Finally, when the dauphin and Jeanne were in "the small chapel," the angel left. Jeanne cried when he disappeared, and she wished her soul had gone with him. No, it was not because of her merits that the angel came. Rather, "he came for a great cause, in the hope that the king would believe the sign and that I no longer be hassled. . . . It pleased God to do so through a simple *pucelle*, to defeat the king's adversaries." The king believed the sign "on the advice of the churchmen and by the sign of the Cross." The churchmen themselves believed it "by their science and because they were learned."

The Letter and the Spirit

Few of Jeanne's biographers have taken the story literally. That an angel brought down a gold crown from heaven looks extraordinary enough; but that the said crown would then not have been preserved as a precious relic is unbelievable. Some have thought the story so fantastic that it must have been entirely made up: Jeanne was either lying or affabulating. But lying was not in her character, and what she could gain from such a lie is not clear at all. Affabulation is, I would think, an acceptable term, if it means that she was able to construe a set of symbols in order to express what could not pass through merely factual language.

For still others, Jeanne was confused. The strain must have been exhausting when she struggled to respond to constant interrogations that jumped from one topic to another without any logic other than that of entrapment and that time and again returned to the same point in order to trip her into giving contradictory answers. But apart from the episode in the cemetery of St.-Ouen and Jeanne's alleged abjuration, to which we will return, there is no evidence that she ever was confused. Jeanne speaks simply and, as the voices repeatedly told her, "coura-geously."[40] She knows what she wants, and it is God's will: to have the dauphin crowned properly at Reims. In Garivel's words, "When Jeanne was asked why she called the king, dauphin, and not king, she said that she would not call him king until he had been crowned and anointed at Reims, in the city where she was decided to lead him."[41]

Another version of this point of view suggests that Jeanne got so involved in her tale that she could no longer distinguish what in it was true and what imagined. She was manipulated by the judges and told them what they wanted to hear, describing objects and images with which they were familiar and which they themselves suggested to her, as has happened in some notorious trials and kidnapping episodes of the twentieth century.[42] Then she would have made the story more and more fantastic as she vainly looked for a way out of it. In a different mood, however, one could entertain the notion that Jeanne was making fun of her judges on the principle that stupid questions deserve stupid answers, or that she was testing their credulity to see how far she could safely go in responding to questions that she had no in-tention of answering. For she often protested that she would be-tray nothing of what she was bound not to divulge.

Comparing the testimonies at Poitiers with Jeanne's own story of the angel with the crown, however, I do not think that Jeanne was confused, or so much under stress that she hardly knew what she was saying, or hopelessly entangled in her crea-tive imagination. The story was a symbolic tale made up on the spur of the moment, that summed up all her work in favor of

---

[40]. . . *hardiment:* 3/13: T, 1:134.

[41]François Garivel: Q, 3:19–20.

[42]Karen Sullivan believes that Jeanne never named the archangel or the two saints until their identity was suggested by the judges; her argumenta-tion leads to farfetched interpretations of what Jeanne is recorded to have said (Wheeler and Wood, *Fresh Verdicts,* 104–5). Other fantastic interpreta-tions are offered in Anne Llewellyin Barstow, *Joan of Arc: Heretic, Mystic, Shaman* (Lewiston: B. Mellen Press, 1986). In reality, the only point where the Rouen tribunal found evidence of heresy was in the wearing of male clothing; and Jeanne was cleared of this by the declaration of nullity, which was itself pronounced by a pontifical commission.

Charles VII. The siege of Orléans had been lifted. The king had been crowned at Reims. The tide of war had turned against the English armies. With the change of fortune that could be observed after the coronation, the policy of the duke of Burgundy became so unpredictable that Jeanne's opinion was quite realistic when she argued with Catherine de la Rochelle, who wanted to "go to the duke of Burgundy to make peace, [that] it seemed to her that one will not find peace there except at the tip of the lance."[43] Jeanne was convinced that the process leading to the coronation had been the fruit of divine intervention and that angels and saints had participated in it. The crown, then, had to be of gold, since it was highly precious. But it was not a traditional crown of metal. It was a spiritual crown. For in Jeanne's view of earthly kingdoms it is the king of heaven who effectively bestows the crown on an earthly dynasty for the protection of the people and the exercise of justice. This is the sense of the painting on her standard. And it is a political principle of the highest order. As Jeanne wrote on July 17, 1429, to the duke of Burgundy when she invited him to go to Reims for the coronation, she was serving "the holy kingdom of France," and she warned him, "All those who make war against the said holy kingdom of France make war against King Jesus, King of Heaven and of all the world, my noble and sovereign Lord."[44]

Not all the courtiers could see the crown, for not all were spiritual enough for the necessary discernment. Not all even, as Jeanne had sensed since her arrival at Chinon, were in favor of entrusting her with the mission she requested. But the facts had proven her true: "My works and my deeds are all in the hand of God and I refer to him. And I assure you that I would want to do or say nothing that is against the Christian faith; and if I had done or said, or if I had something on my body, that the clerics could say is against the Christian faith that Our Lord has established, I would not sustain it but I would throw it out."[45]

[43] 3/3: T, 1:105.
[44] Q, 5:126–127.
[45] T, 1:158.

In spite of its twists and turns, the story of the crown contains a straightforward lesson. Jeanne lived in two worlds at the same time, on earth with its miseries and struggles and in what she called paradise with the angels and saints of God. The second world was as real to her as the first. In terms of their objective dignity, however, the kingdom of paradise was first and earth was second. Everything that is good on earth reflects something of heaven. The kingdoms of this world, especially the Christian kingdoms, should be images of the kingdom of heaven. That is why it was so important to restore the proper order of society in France. Thus Jeanne's inner life is inseparable from her actions. Familiarity with the angels and saints of paradise must bear fruit in the works of justice.

FIVE

Jeanne's Saints

In the early fifteenth century the process of official canonization by the Bishop of Rome was not very old. Before the end of the tenth century canonization had been a matter of public renown for holiness and of more-or-less spontaneous popular devotion rather than a formal exercise of discernment and authority at the episcopal or primatial level. Standards of holiness that were operative in canonization were unclear. Emperor Charlemagne, with his numerous concubines, was by no means a model of virtue. Yet he could be honored as a saint in some parts of France—and by Jeanne *la Pucelle* herself[1]—while ignored in Rome. By the same token, saints were known and venerated locally rather than universally. The spreading of devotion from the local level to the universal was slow and uncertain. On January 31, 998, however, the first pontifical canonization was celebrated, when John XVI (pope, 985–98) canonized Ulrich of Augsburg at a conclave of his cardinals. This action was made public on February 3. From then on, beatifications and canonizations were less likely to result from local interests, and standards for official recognition could be established that applied in the entire Latin Church.

Yet there was a reverse to the picture. First, no one could be proclaimed a saint unless the fame of that person's virtues had reached the Holy See. Second, it became clearer than ever that sainthood did not equate with holiness: Many holy persons

---

[1]Jeanne declared that Orléans had been liberated, not by her but by God, through the intercession of St. Louis and St. Charlemagne, the two of them being former sovereigns of the country, often set up as models for their successors (Dunois: Q, 1:6).

would never be officially recognized to be such. In these conditions attempts at canonization could easily fail. Official sainthood relied in part on the attraction the image of a holy person exercised on popular imagination. In this the voice of the people was paramount. But a long time could elapse between a local renown for holiness and a formal decision by the Bishop of Rome. The proclamation of a person as a saint in the universal Church was bound to remain not only slow but also rare.

By the time of Jeanne the process of canonization in the Western Church had become fairly homogeneous and centralized. There was an unavoidable imbalance in the process: more clergy than laity were canonized, more popes than bishops of any other see, more men than women, more single Christians than married. The liturgical calendar made room for a fairly extensive sanctoral approved at the several levels of authority: diocesan, provincial or metropolitan, national, patriarchal, and primatial. In principle this marked the limits of public devotion. The influence of the Roman liturgy on outlying dioceses tended to focus the celebrations on the saints who were honored in Rome. But pilgrims who traveled to distant shrines exported their home devotions, and they eventually brought others back.

The cult of relics, extensive through the Middle Ages and the Renaissance, thrived on the desire to have recognizable tokens that the communion of saints does include the two worlds of the present life and heaven. And the ensuing commerce in remains of the saints was not without influence on local practices. In the Lorraine of Jeanne Darc the cult of St. Nicholas, an Oriental bishop who had no special claim to popularity in the duchy or the bishoprics, flourished largely through the importation of a relic from the Italian city of Bari. This relic was venerated in the church of St.-Nicolas-de-Port. But devotion to saints could be a vestige of political entities that were no longer in existence. The veneration of St. Nicholas followed a north-south line from the Netherlands to southern Italy, an area that corresponded to the Lotharingia of the Carolingians.

In the liturgy the saints were honored rather than invoked. Their life and death provided an occasion to give glory to God. Yet it was inevitable that persons in distress would privately invoke the saints, asking for their prayer and assistance. The popular invocation of saints bypassed a number of theological questions: do the saints, who are now in the heavenly kingdom of God, hear us down below? do they have direct power on earth, or is their action limited to praying for us? In the absence of clear biblical teaching, imagination could assign to the saints more influence on earth than is warranted. The saints that Jeanne knew were therefore those of the liturgical calendar, and among them, she knew best those who had been given monuments or were somehow represented in the upper valley of the Meuse river where she had lived in her recent childhood. Generally speaking, John the Baptist was the most celebrated saint in the Middle Ages after the Mother of God. Many churches were named after him, and his name was frequently given in baptism, both in the masculine and the feminine form. Jeanne got her Christian name from him.

The Visions

Yet neither the Baptist nor the Virgin Mary was ever seen by Jeanne *la Pucelle*. Here again she was a child of her times. The recorded apparitions of the Virgin in the Middle Ages are relatively few, and most of them have come in the form of late legends composed to illustrate somebody's life. Stories of apparitions belonged to the hagiographic genre, along with stories of miraculous interventions. They seldom tried to be credible. The most reasonable tended to be related to the origin or the reform of religious orders, which precisely had the means to spread them. This was the case at Cluny with Hugh of Semur (d. 1109), among the Premonstratentians with St. Norbert in 1120, around Cîteaux with Robert de Molesmes in 1098 and St. Bernard (d. 1153), in the Order of Preachers with St. Dominic (1170–1221), among the Mercedarians with St. Peter Nolasco (1218), among Franciscans with St. Francis of Assisi (ca. 1182–1226), in the old Carmel with St. Simon Stock in 1251. Such stories illustrated the founding of the Servites in 1233.

The Virgin Mary was not, as she became in the nineteenth century, the chief object of spiritual visions. She was, of course, celebrated in the liturgy, notably at the four feasts of her Purification, her Nativity, the Annunciation by the archangel Gabriel,

and her Assumption into heaven. Poets wrote about the Mother
of Christ. Statues and images of her were everywhere to be seen.
She was featured in the illuminations of manuscripts. There were
spiritual and theological authors who themselves designed the
pictures that should illustrate their writings. Hildegard of Bingen
(1098–1179) showed the Virgin in a variation of the traditional
theme of *deisis,* attending the Holy Trinity on one side, the
apostle John on the other side.[2] Hildegard also depicted Mary as
the highest of the saints, sitting on a royal throne with the adornments of a queen, the Queen of Heaven.[3] In these conditions it
may seem surprising that Mary was not credited with many apparitions. Among those who were thought to have had visions of
the Virgin Mary were some béguines and nuns in Flanders and
the Netherlands, such as Juette de Huy (d. 1228),[4] Julienne du
Mont-Cornillon (d. 1258), and several of the great women mystics of the German lands, like Elizabeth of Schönau (d. 1164).
St. Brigid of Sweden (d. 1373) believed that she had been shown
many events of the life of Mary. There were even bishops at the
Council of Basle who wanted to canonize her visions and put
their account on a par with the Gospels. But it is noteworthy
that, against the opinion of the master of the sacred palace Juan
de Torquemada (1388–1468), Chancellor Jean Gerson rejected
their authenticity, while along with the archbishop of Embrun,
Jacques Gélu (d. 1442), he defended the value of Jeanne *la Pucelle*'s spiritual experience as early as 1429, in her very lifetime.[5]

Since visions of Mary were rare, it fits the spiritual image of
Jeanne *la Pucelle* that the Mother of God would not be among
her heavenly visitors. Jeanne had no discernible connection with
religious orders or religious reform, in spite of the wild hypothesis that she was a Franciscan Tertiary and had dealings with St.
Colette. The upper Meuse valley held no important abbey or pri-
ory of women. There is no suggestion in what is reported of her

[2]Matthew Fox, ed., *Illuminations of Hildegard of Bingen* (Santa Fe:
Bear & Co., 1985) facing page 111.

[3]Ibid., facing page 115.

[4]Cited in Barnay, *Les Apparitions,* 62.

[5]Gerson, "De puella aurelianensi," in Jean Gerson, *Oeuvres complètes*
(Paris: Desclée, 1961) 661–65; Jacques Gélu, "Tractatus de puella," Q,
3:393–421.

that, pious though she was, she ever considered the religious life as a possible vocation for herself. Her parents did not, since they attempted to marry her off. That marriage was against her wishes they had no way of knowing at the time, since she did not tell anyone before going to Chinon that she had promised to keep her virginity for as long as it would please God.

The only preparation Jeanne may have had for visionary experiences of saints was the attention she paid as a child to their pictures and statues. Presumably she would not have been acquainted with manuscript illuminations. But she had to know the statues, paintings, and decorated windows of the churches and chapels where she prayed. She frequented the churches of Domremy, Greux, Maxey. Michel Lebuin remembered that she went at least once a week to the chapel of Notre-Dame de Bermont: "Jeanne went willingly to church and frequented holy places. I know, for when I was young I went several times with her on pilgrimage to the hermitage of Notre-Dame de Bermont; she went to that hermitage every Saturday with her sisters and she lighted candles."[6] Others confirmed that she often went there to pray, sometimes taking candles with her.[7] Through the woods Bermont is about two kilometers from her home. It was just a small chapel in a clearing with presumably a small building for an occasional hermit.[8] As the inside walls of churches and chapels were usually painted, Jeanne was undoubtedly well acquainted with images, not only of the archangel Michael but also of St. Catherine and St. Marguerite. Naturally she knew about St. Remi, the patron saint of her village, about St. Nicholas, the patron of Lorraine. She must have felt toward the Virgin Mary the filial piety that was appropriate to the Mother of God. As the witnesses of her childhood often testified, she was indeed devoted to St. Mary. Yet the only heavenly personages whom she identified as speaking with her were two traditional saints with whom, in a sense, she was easily familiar, St. Catherine and St. Marguerite.

[6]Q, 2:439–40.

[7]Among others, Jean Waterin (Q, 2:419–20), Zabillet Gérardin (426–27); Colin Colin (433).

[8]Today the chapel is part of a larger structure that looks like a medium-sized farmhouse; there is an official pilgrimage in July.

Jeanne's Two Saints

Catherine of Alexandria, virgin and martyr, a victim of the persecution of Emperor Maxentius in 305, was a popular saint. She was thought to be of royal blood. Her legend made her the special protectress of philosophers and students: she discussed at length with all the sages of pagan Egypt about the Christian faith. Jeanne's elder sister was named Catherine.[9] Pictures and statues of the saint usually showed her standing next to a wheel. This was a reference to the form of her martyrdom, as she was exposed on the wheel, an old form of torture, before being beheaded. In symbolic imagination this made her the patron saint of wheelwrights. Her youth and virginity made her also a model for young unmarried women, and this may have had a special attraction for Jeanne even before she decided to keep her virginity. St. Catherine's feast day, November 25, was observed as a holy day of obligation in many a diocese. The church of Maxey, the village on the right bank of the Meuse, in the duchy, was dedicated to St. Catherine. As borders were not guarded it was easy to walk to it. There also was a St. Catherine chapel a short distance from Maxey, cared for by the canons of Brixey-sur-Vaux. Jeanne may well have seen it, too.

Marguerite of Antioch, a shepherdess, also virgin and martyr, was believed to be a martyr of the persecution of Diocletian, which started in the year 303. She would have been condemned by an official named Olibrius, whose advances Marguerite would have rejected. The patron saint of expectant women about to give birth, she was commonly shown holding a sword, the instrument of her beheading, and standing near a dragon, symbolic of the devils over which she triumphed. Her feast was celebrated on July 20. An old statue of her believed to date back to the fifteenth century can still be seen in the church of Domremy. If it was there at the time, Jeanne must have prayed in front of it.

---

[9]Most authors agree that Catherine was older than Jeanne, married, and already deceased before Jeanne's departure. Yet after the coronation Jeanne spoke with nostalgia of returning to Domremy, where she would watch the sheep "with my sister and my brother" (Q, 3:15–16). She may have had a younger sister whose name is not known.

Both Catherine and Marguerite belong to the group of fourteen "auxiliary saints" or "Holy Helpers," whose intercession for specific purposes was popularly believed, especially in German lands, to be particularly efficacious, the other auxiliary saints being George, Blaise, Erasmus, Pantaleon, Vitus, Christopher, Denys, Cyriacus, Acacius, Eustace, Giles, and Barbara. Devotion to these saints is documented in the first years of the fourteenth century in the regions of Regensburg and Bamberg, from where it spread chiefly to the Germanies, Hungary, and Sweden.[10] It is not impossible that Jeanne knew of this kind of piety, for local priests and the occasional Franciscan preacher may have preached about it. Yet even if these saints were famous in some parts of Christendom for the favors they brought to their devotees, Jeanne never expressed any special devotion to any of them except Catherine and Marguerite. The way of her piety, as is manifest in her sayings and her actions, did not go in that direction. She was not interested in special favors. When Jeanne invoked Catherine and Marguerite as she did in prison she did not ask for privileges. She requested their spiritual assistance and advice in bearing her sufferings, and she begged them to bring her prayers to the Lord Christ. She understood angels and saints precisely to be agents of Christ, the king of heaven.

Questions About Saints

It is not clear whether the two saints appeared distinctly to Jeanne before she went to war. From the beginning of her visions there was light, plenty of light. In her captivity, the light, as Jeanne spoke of it, was focused on the two women saints who came to guide and protect her. When she spoke of her military campaign Jeanne related the saints to intimations of her sufferings—her being wounded at Orléans, being captured, jumping from the window at Beaurevoir—rather than to moments of success. And she described them with the same alternance of precision and vagueness that she used for the archangel.

[10]In 1446 a shepherd in Franconia was credited with a vision of Jesus assisted by fourteen saints; in 1503 Mathis Grünewald painted a retable showing the fourteen saints (now at Lindenhart, Germany).

On March 15 she admitted that she often made reverence to her saints when they came to her, though not as much as they deserve, and that she had asked them to forgive her for that. Yet this followed no absolute rule. In prison when the voice woke her up on February 24 she simply sat up in bed and joined her hands.[11] Asked if she had not also offered them "lighted candles or other things, or had Masses said,"[12] she responded: "No, except having Mass said by the hand of the priest in honor of St. Catherine; I believe that she is indeed one of those who have appeared to me; and I have not lighted as many candles as I would wish for St. Catherine and St. Marguerite who are in Paradise; but I firmly believe that they are the ones who come to me." She does this "in honor of God, of Our Lady, and of St. Catherine who is in heaven; and I make no difference between St. Catherine who is in heaven and the one who reveals herself to me." She firmly believes that her visitors—voices and faces—are indeed from heaven, and she knows their identity from what they themselves have said.

In the afternoon of March 17, a Saturday, Jeanne was pushed further about the saints by an unnamed judge. She used to wear two rings. On one of them, given to her by her parents, the words *Jhesus Maria* were inscribed. It was not a ring of fine gold, Jeanne remarked, it could have been brass.[13] There was no precious stone in it. The names of Jesus and Mary were on it, but Jeanne did not know who had inscribed the words. The ring had been given to Jeanne by her mother. It had been taken from her by Burgundians. Her other ring was a gift of one of her brothers, and the bishop of Beauvais had stolen it.[14] As Jeanne easily

[11]T, 1:58, with a reference to it in article 10, p. 203.
[12]T, 1:159–60.
[13]T, 1:176–77.
[14]T, 1:84–85. A judge asked: "And you, Jeanne, did you wear rings?" Jeanne, ever swift, turned to the bishop: "You took one from me. Give it back. The Burgundians have another. If you have it, show it to me." Who gave her the ring that the Burgundians have? "My father or my mother. The names of Jesus and Mary must have been written on it. I do not know who engraved it; there was no precious stone, if I remember well. The ring was given to me at Domremy. My brother gave me another, that you have, and you should give it to a church."

perceived, the judges were suspicious of rings. The marks on them might have magic significance. But Jeanne anticipated their objection: "I have never healed anyone with my rings." When she looked at her parents' gift it was both for pleasure and to honor her father and mother. With the ring on her finger she had indeed touched St. Catherine.

This touching of the saint occasioned a series of insidious questions:

> *Question:* What part [did you touch]?
> *Answer:* You will have nothing more.
> *Q:* Have you ever kissed or hugged the saints Catherine and Marguerite?
> *A:* I have hugged both of them.
> *Q:* Was their smell good?
> *A:* It is good to know;[15] their smell was good.
> *Q:* When you hugged them did you feel heat or anything else?
> *A:* I could not hug them without feeling and touching them.
> *Q:* In what part did you hug them, above or below?
> *A:* It is more proper to hug them below than above.[16]
> *Q:* Have you ever offered them wreaths?
> *A:* Several times in their honor I have offered wreaths to their images or memorials in churches; and to those that appeared I did not offer any that I remember. . . .
> *Q:* When the saints came to you did you make reverence to them, genuflecting or bowing?
> *A:* Yes, and as much as I could make reverence to them I did so. I know that they are those who are in the kingdom of paradise.[17]

Jeanne did not normally see the entire figure of the saints. Often she saw only their head. The responses she gave on March 1 are particularly significant. The two saints come to her every day, and "always in the same shape; their heads are crowned with very rich crowns. As to their robes I know nothing."[18] But how

---

[15] *Il est bon à savoir* (Latin, *hoc bonum est scire*), an expression that Jeanne uses occasionally, carries the connotation of self-evidence.

[16] The question meant, "did you hug their knees or their face?" It is recorded that on occasion Jeanne knelt before Charles VII and embraced his knees. Such an homage was appropriate for the saints.

[17] T, 1:176–78.

[18] T, 1:84.

can she distinguish if "the thing that appears to her is man or woman?"

> *A:* I know and recognize them well from their voices and because they reveal themselves, and I know nothing that has not been done by God's revelation and precept. . . .
>
> *Q:* What kind of a figure do you see?
>
> *A:* Their face.
>
> *Q:* Do the saints who appear have hair?
>
> *A:* It is good to know!
>
> *Q:* Is there something between the crowns and the hair?
>
> *A:* No.
>
> *Q:* Is their hair long and flowing?
>
> *A:* I know nothing of that. I do not know if there was something like arms or if other parts were shown. They spoke very well and beautifully, and I understood them very well.
>
> *Q:* How did they speak if they had no parts?
>
> *A:* I refer on God. Their voice is beautiful, sweet, and humble, and speaks the Gallic language.
>
> *Q:* Does not St. Marguerite speak the English language?
>
> *A:* Why should she speak English when she is not of the English party?
>
> *Q:* On those heads, with the crowns were there rings at their ears or elsewhere?
>
> *A:* I know nothing of that.

The judge was of course hinting that Jeanne had seen the heads of devils, with horns between hair and crown. Had she said that she saw the whole figure of the saints, he could have asked her to describe their feet and suggested that they also had a tail.

However this may be, Jeanne's responses on those two days of March 1 and March 17 indicate the nature of her visions. What she sees in the apparitions is what she already knows from Christian art: The heads of the saints wear a crown of glory. But what is determinative for her is not the sight she sees; it is the words she hears, the message communicated, for this message comes from no other than God.

Voices in Captivity

In the period of Jeanne's captivity the two saints appear frequently. St. Catherine is the leader, the one who speaks, but she is usually assisted by St. Marguerite. In their mission to her the saints act as the archangel's agents. To Jean de la Fontaine, Jeanne denied that the angel had failed her "in regard to luck" when she was captured: "I believe that once it pleased God it was better for me to be taken."[19] She also denied that the archangel had ever failed her "in regard to graces," for he comforts her every day through St. Catherine and St. Marguerite.

Catherine sometimes comes only as a voice, sometimes as a vision and a voice. On Tuesday, March 13, Jean le Maistre interrupted the story of the crown to ask if Jeanne had spoken with St. Catherine since the previous day. She answered: "Since yesterday I have heard her; she has told me several times to respond boldly to the judges on what they would ask me concerning the trial." At other times St. Catherine was seen as well as heard. Together the two saints, with the occasional presence of Michael and at least once of Gabriel, constitute what Jeanne designates as her counsel,[20] on which it is safer to rely than on the king's counsel or the decisions of military leaders. The heart of the saints' message is twofold: The dauphin will recover his kingdom,[21] and they will lead Jeanne to paradise.

In her military campaigns the saints acted as trusted advisers. In the sufferings of what Jeanne called her "martyrdom," they came as companions and consolers:

> St. Catherine told me that I would be helped; I do not know if this will be by being freed from prison or if during the trial there will take place some turmoil through which I could be freed. Most often my voices tell me that I will be freed through a great victory; and afterwards they say: 'Accept everything, do not be concerned about your martyrdom, you will come at the end to the kingdom of Paradise.' I call it martyrdom on account of the pain and adversity I suffer in my prison, and I do not know if I will suffer more; but I rely on Our Lord.[22]

[19]T, 1:122.

[20]Jeanne uses the French word *conseil* (*consilium* in Latin, not *concilium*) in its two senses: a piece of advice, and an advisory committee. Thus *sine consilio vocum suarum* translates *sans le conseil de ses voix* (3/15, T, 1:160), *suum consilium secretum* translates *mon conseil secret* (2/21, T, 1:38).

[21]T, 1:86.

[22]T, 1:148.

The saints often come without her asking. But if they stay away too long Jeanne prays the Lord to send them, and they come. They have always been present when she needed them.[23] "St. Catherine responds immediately, though sometimes I cannot hear her well because of the movement of people and the noises of the guards. When I make a request from St. Catherine, right away she and St. Marguerite make a request from Our Lord, and then by Our Lord's command they give me the response."[24] A promise made to them is made to the Lord.[25] The saints are present at all important moments. They attended the angel with the crown as far as the king's chamber.[26]

Spiritual Freedom

The voices did not dictate everything that Jeanne did, and they left her free to take their advice or not. At Domremy they "left it to her to speak to my father and mother, or not to tell." At Beaurevoir when she jumped through a window she acted in spite of their advice.[27] Jeanne's prayer to them generally turned on three points: "first, my campaign; then, that God may help the French and protect well the cities in their obedience; and finally the salvation of my soul."[28] That is, she asks for light and she prays for the fulfillment of her God-given mission, for the people, and for herself. Jeanne is evidently convinced that her counsel is from God. The saints "do not command anything without the good will of Our Lord."[29] Jeanne affirmed that she had always followed their advice except when she leapt through a window in one of her attempts to escape. Even then, however, the saints protected her, for though she was sore and stunned by the fall she was not killed. She admitted that it was a sin to jump, though not in itself, only because St. Catherine had told her not

[23]T, 1:122.
[24]T, 1:146.
[25]T, 1:123.
[26]T, 1:138.
[27]T, 1:144.
[28]T, 1:147.
[29]T, 1:160.

to do it. Catherine blamed her and told her to confess it to a priest.[30] But it was not, as the judges thought, an attempted suicide. She only wanted to go back to Compiègne, for she had heard that the good people of the city were in danger of being massacred, and she would have preferred to die with them than to be sold to the English.[31] Asked by her questioner if the jump was a mortal sin, she answered: "I do not know; I rely on Our Lord." Jeanne's basic point was that a prisoner has a natural right to escape. She was always clear about her right to freedom. At the first public session of the trial Bishop Cauchon had ruled that "it was forbidden to her to leave the prison without his agreement." But she had retorted: "I accept no interdiction. If I escaped no one could accuse me of not keeping my word, for I have never given my word to anyone. And I protest against the chains and irons in which I have been placed. . . . Every prisoner has a right to escape."[32] Going through the front door had failed her at Beaulieu. So she tried jumping through a window, but the window was too high to make it to freedom.

Light on this World

From time to time Jeanne's counsel brought her specific information. It told her many things that were destined to the king (and Jeanne pointedly adds, not to the bishop of Beauvais!).[33] It advised her about what should be painted on her standard.[34] It told her that "the story of Catherine de la Rochelle was nothing."[35] Likewise it provided Jeanne with foreknowledge of a few events, or perhaps only with unusual insights: She knew that she would be wounded at Orléans and would bleed above her breast;[36] she knew that she would be captured.[37]

[30]T, 1:145.
[31]T, 1:144-46.
[32]T, 1:42.
[33]T, 1:60.
[34]T, 1:114.
[35]T, 1:116.
[36]Pasquerel: Q, 3:393-404.
[37]T, 1:111-12.

The saints brought Jeanne certitude not only that Orléans would be liberated but also about various details of the battle. On May 8 the English army that was besieging Orléans lined up for a formal battle. This was their preferred form of combat, when their archers could function the most effectively. At Crécy and Azincourt their tactic had inflicted disaster on the French. An all-out fight in the open was swifter than starving a city to surrender or attempting to scale the walls of a fortress, strategies in which their archers' skills could hardly be used. After losing Fort Les Tourelles, the English commanders were clearly hoping they could taunt the French into the open fields and a pitched battle. The French commanders did line up their troops facing the enemy and some wanted to launch the attack. Yet Jeanne opposed it, for she had been promised by her voices that the English would soon retreat. Then suddenly the English army withdrew in good order and left the scene.

Jeanne's counsel affirmed that Charles would be crowned at Reims and that the duke of Orléans would return from England. Jeanne may have understood, though this was not in their messages, that she would contribute directly to the duke's freedom. Jean d'Alençon reported that "she said she had received four tasks: to drive the English out, to have the king crowned and annointed in Reims, to free the duke of Orléans from English hands, and to lift the siege of Orléans."[38] How would she obtain his freedom? She projected to take enough prisoners to raise the money for the duke's ransom: "I would have captured enough of the English to have him back; and if I had not enough I would have gone over the sea to fetch him in England by force."[39] The voices had told her so. In turn she had told the king. But to achieve this she would have needed about three years or perhaps a little less: "If I had lasted three years without obstacle, I would have liberated him. Actually, the delay was less than three years, and more than one; I do not remember for the moment."[40] And Jeanne knew, or at least she suspected, that she had little time ahead of her. Jean d'Alençon testified: "I some-

[38]Q, 3:98–99.
[39]T, 1:128.
[40]T, 1:129.

times heard Jeanne tell the king that she would last one year, not much more, and that one should work hard during that year."[41]

In fact, however, if indeed Charles d'Orléans was a prisoner in England since Azincourt, the English leaders did not agree to a ransom before the conference of Arras between representatives of Charles VII and Henry VI in the summer of 1435. They followed a policy of total surrender that led to the undoing of their cause. It was chiefly their refusal to settle anything short of obtaining the crown of France for Henry VI that persuaded the duke of Burgundy, Philippe *le Bon,* to withdraw his pledge to the king of England and, reversing his alliances, to join forces with Charles VII. In this case, the discrepancy between Jeanne's expectations and the political reality is patent. But the source of the discrepancy was, first, that Jeanne's voices did not dictate all of her conduct and never briefed her completely concerning the dynastic struggle. It was, second, that Jeanne was never forced to do anything. She always remained entirely free to take advice or not. She always followed her voices, she said, with the exception of her attempt to escape the castle of Beaurevoir.

It was the saints who warned Jeanne that "she would be captured before the feast of St. John, and that it had to be so, that she should not be surprised but should accept it all, and that God would help her."[42] This took place in the ditches of Melun, during the Easter week of 1429. But no detail was given as to the place or the time. Had she known more, Jeanne declared, she would not have gone there, though she immediately corrected herself: "Had I known the time, and that I would be taken, I would not have gone willingly; yet in the end I would have done what they commanded, happen what may." Jeanne's whole being was to do the will of God.

Light on the Spiritual World

Jeanne *la Pucelle* was smart enough to guess that the tribunal of Rouen was trying to get her to say something about the saints that would somehow contradict Christian orthodoxy. Yet

[41]Q, 3:98–99.
[42]T, 1:111–12.

she never altered her story, and her attitude to her voices did not change even when she was led by the questioning to provide precisions that may well have been afterthoughts on her part. The two saints that speak to her come from the kingdom of paradise. They are sent by Jesus, the king of heaven, to do the divine will in the kingdom of France. At this point we touch on what may be called, with a somewhat grand term, the politics of Jeanne *la Pucelle*. If indeed the real king of France is Christ himself, the earthly king and his kingdom have a sacramental dimension that must be respected. The king represents Christ. And it is essentially for this reason that he must be properly crowned by the archbishop of Reims in his own cathedral with the oil of the *sainte ampoule*. The heart of Jeanne's task was to restore their sacramental dimension to these earthly realities, though this, of course, was not the language she used.

In the difficult circumstances of the war that has been caused by the ambition of the Lancastrian dynasty God is free to choose the means that will restore the proper order. After her first days of surprise Jeanne realized that she was chosen for that purpose. That she became Jeanne *la Pucelle* precisely expressed her acceptance of God's will. The role of the saints Catherine and Marguerite was to assist her in this task, as it had been that of the archangel Michael to reveal the essentials of her mission. Jeanne therefore always maintained that the angels and saints who spoke to her were from God: "The voice comes from God, and I believe I will not tell you all simply what I know. And I am more afraid of failing by saying something that displeases these voices than of answering you."[43] Since the saints came from God and sent her on her way, then she also came from God. Jeanne affirmed it unambiguously in a heated exchange when Cauchon insisted that she must take the oath of telling the truth in a form she did not like: "I have come from God and I have nothing to do here. Send me back to God from whom I have come!"[44]

When, on May 2, Jean de Châtillon admonished her to submit to the Church in regard to six points that were to be the basis of the official accusations, he asked if she made the sign of

[43]T, 1:60.
[44]T, 1:56–57.

the Cross when St. Catherine and St. Marguerite came to her. She was noncommittal, saying evasively, in what French folklore calls the Normand fashion, "sometimes yes, sometimes no."[45] Jeanne of course was aware of being in Normandy, and she was not devoid of humor. But when asked further if she had anything to add concerning her revelations, her response was totally transparent: "I rely on my Judge, who is God; my revelations are from God, without any intermediary."[46] As is the case in regard to the angels, Jeanne's devotion to the saints who visit her illustrates her spiritual way. God has given her insights into the spiritual world to which most humans remain blind, even though that world is more real than the visible world of everyday. But no one can understand this unless a similar insight has been granted. And it is not given to every Christian believer to have glimpses of the angels and saints who now live in the kingdom of paradise, of which Christ is the unquestioned Lord.

Jeanne Among Warriors

When they heard Jeanne's story, many of the partisans of Charles VII were inclined to believe her. Others suspended their judgment while they agreed to humor her and even support her in what she wanted to do, provided it seemed reasonable enough to their practical minds. Among Charles VII's advisers, neither the favorite, La Trémoille, nor the archbishop of Reims, Regnault de Chartres, really believed that Jeanne talked with angels and saints. Yet they could go along with her plans as long as these seemed to work. The high command of the armies had of course a considerable experience of war. In fact, they remained in charge of the fighting. Jean, comte de Dunois, called *le bâtard d'Orléans* (1403–1468), the *connétable* Arthur de Richemont, comte de Bretagne (1393–1458), Gilles de Laval, seigneur de Rais (1404–1440), Etienne de Vignoles, nicknamed La Hire (ca. 1390–1444), Poton de Xaintrailles (d. 1461), never relinquished

---

[45]T, 1:346. More exactly, the Normand fashion would be, "Maybe yes, maybe no!" But this is suggested by Jeanne's words.

[46]T, 1:345. *Je m'en rapporte à* . . . is Jeanne's frequent expression. It can be rendered "I rely on . . . ," "I refer to . . ." There is a connotation of trust that is not fully rendered by the English words.

their command into her hand. Nor was there any hint from the king that they should do so. Most of the armies that fought for Charles VII did not belong to him or to the nation. They went with their commander. These held their own councils of war, with or without Jeanne. They were indeed prepared to listen to her but also to argue. They would not trust her advice unless they could see that it made strategic or tactical sense. The responsibility of victory or defeat was theirs. Nothing that angels or saints could say or do could alter this. In these conditions Jeanne acted as their spiritual adviser, not as a commander. The men of lesser rank who had led her to the king—Bertrand de Poulengy[47] and Jean de Nouillonpont—learned from living with her for eleven days to accept her views unquestioningly. The members of her military house, chiefly Jean d'Aulon and her page Jean de Coute, learned not to question her insights, though they may have felt inclined to protect her from possible harm that she tended to overlook. Jeanne was correct when, on February 22, she denied having said that she was *chef de guerre* in her letter to the king of England, the duke of Bedford, and the other English soldiers.[48] She radiated a spiritual light and she was a spiritual force, not a warlord.

Seen from the English side, however, Jeanne's alleged familiarity with angels and saints made no sense. In the eyes of the duke of Bedford her claims were all lies and delusion. As the duke wrote to his nephew the king, Jeanne was "a disciple and limb of the Fiend, . . . that used false enchantments and sorcery"[49] to win her battles. It was she who had reversed the course

---

[47]The name Poulengy may be identical with Pulligny, a small village south of Nancy that appears in the story of Claude des Armoises: see appendix B.

[48]T, 1:221. She also denied dictating that French cities must be surrendered to her (instead of to the king) and that she was sent by God to throw the English out of France *corps pour corps* (literally, "body for body," meaning something like "in hand to hand combat"); she commented that "if the English had believed this letter they would have acted wisely, and they will find it out before seven years."

[49]Q, 5:136. A decree from the duke of Gloucester against soldiers who refused to go to France, presumably because they were afraid of witchcraft, is dated May 3, 1430 (Q, 5:162–64).

of the war and put an end to the English army's stream of victories. The duke, I would judge, was the one person in authority who really hated her with an implacable hatred. He was the one who had bought her from Jean de Luxembourg and provided for the trial over which Cauchon had agreed to preside. It was for the sake of his politics that Jeanne had to be denounced as a witch and, in order for her to be burned, to be condemned as a heretic and to be pushed to recantation and relapse.

As to the churchmen who sat in judgment over Jeanne's voices, they would pretend to see in her deeds and words blasphemies against the dignity of angels and saints. If Jeanne was in good faith she was mistaken; but in their eyes it was more likely that either she was, like Catherine de la Rochelle, an impostor who lied when she declared that she had divine guidance, or else a witch who, as she consorted with devils, was able to entrap her foes in magic spells. Of course the judges at Rouen knew, intellectually, about the kingdom of God in heaven. But after siding with the Lancastrian politics of the English party they would not concede that the politics of God could possibly be against them. And it is obvious that their personal life did not share Jeanne's experience of living on earth in the companionship of those who are in heaven. The promoter Jean d'Estivet expressed the hidden thoughts of others among them when he threw insults to her face: *paillarde, putain, ordure.*[50] Whether these terms came naturally to a vulgar mind or were a deliberate cruelty meant to hurt her, such language cut into Jeanne's very soul, for it contradicted what her angelic name affirmed. Like the insults of some English soldiers from Fort Les Tourelles—*la putain des Armagnacs*[51]—d'Estivet's insulting language implied that Jeanne was not, as she claimed to be, a virgin and that she could not possibly be "daughter of God."

The Articles of Accusation

The members of the tribunal, and first of all, presumably, its president and chief mover, the bishop of Beauvais, must have

[50]Jean Tiphaine (Q, 3:48–49); Guillaume de la Chambre (52); Guillaume Colles (162).
[51]Pasquerel: Q, 2:101.

felt that Jeanne's position was particularly vulnerable precisely from what she said about angels and saints, for they gave prominence to her alleged conversations with them in the articles of accusation. A list of seventy articles was read to Jeanne on March 28, Wednesday in Holy Week.

Articles 48 to 50 related to her voices: Jeanne believed with temerity "that the voices came from angels, archangels, and saints of God" (art. 48), but in reality she practiced idolatry and made a pact with demons (art. 49), and she invoked demons (art. 50).[52] Jeanne retorted that she had already answered and that she would "call them to her aid as long as she would live." When one of the judges wanted to know exactly how she called them, she said: "I pray Our Lord and Our Lady that they [the saints] send me aid and comfort, and then they send them to me." Being pushed further for the very words she used, she formulated this simple prayer:

> Most sweet God, in honor of your holy passion, I beg you, if you love me, to reveal to me how I must respond to these churchmen. As for the dress, I know well the command by which I have taken it; but I do not know in what way I must leave it. May it therefore please you to teach it to me.[53]

Jeanne then volunteered the information that the voices had already come to her three times that very day, that she heard them well, and that they told her "how to answer about her dress." After article 51 she repeated, "I know well that I was never wounded without receiving great comfort from Our Lord, St. Catherine, and St. Marguerite."[54]

In the next few weeks the seventy articles were reduced in number and carefully reworded. On May 2, an informal list of six articles served as the basis of Jean de Châtillon's charitable admonition to Jeanne.[55] The threat of torture, on May 9, was made on the background of these six articles. But when the final list of accusations was presented to Jeanne on Wednesday, May 23, it had grown to twelve points. The formulation was more careful

[52]Q, 1:112.
[53]T, 1:252. This prayer is at the heart of Pernoud, *La Spiritualité*.
[54]T, 1:255.
[55]T, 1:337–42.

and infinitely more damaging for the accused than the repetitive charges of the seventy points. In the first place Cauchon had taken time for extensive consultation. The twelve articles had been submitted to the University of Paris, and they had come back with the university's judgment on the evidence it had received: Jeanne was found guilty on all points. In the second place, no further explanations were now needed. The articles were no longer mere charges of which Jeanne was accused. In keeping with the normal procedure of the Inquisition they embodied the tribunal's final determination of her guilt. The only item missing was the sentence.

Jeanne's two saints feature more prominently in the twelve articles than in the original seventy:

Article one, as regards the modes and purpose of her apparitions, the subject matter of her revelations, and the quality of Jeanne's person, "the clerics of the University of Paris and others" have concluded that "they are mendacious fiction, seductive, and pernicious, that these revelations and apparitions are superstitions, proceeding from evil and diabolical spirits."[56]

Article two, declares that the story of the angel and the crown, in which the angel is attended by a multitude of angels, some with wings, others with crowns, along with St. Catherine and St. Marguerite, "is not likely to be true but is a presumptuous, seductive, and pernicious lie, a fictitious affair, offensive to the angelic dignity."

Article three, concerning the advice given by angels and saints, the claim that their deeds and words are good, and Jeanne's confession that she "believes it as firmly as she has faith in Christ": these are not sufficient signs to know the above-named angels and saints: "You have believed it lightly and affirmed it with temerity; and moreover, regarding the comparison you make, believing it as firmly etc., you err in faith, *tu erras in fide.*"

Article four, concerning an alleged knowledge of events, secrets, and never previously seen persons, and this through the voices of St. Catherine and St. Marguerite. . . : "The clerics say that this is superstition, divination, presumptuous assertion, and vacuous boasting."

---

[56]T, 1:375–76. The following articles are on pages 376–80.

Article nine, concerning the two saints' promise that they will lead Jeanne to Paradise, and her belief that she has not committed mortal sin. . . . : This is "a presumptuous and excessive assertion, a pernicious lie; it is contrary to your previous assertions, and moreover you have an erroneous understanding of the Christian faith."

Article eleven, concerning the apparitions in general and Jeanne's belief in them. . . : "The clerics say that assuming you have had the revelations and apparitions of which you have boasted in the modes that you have said, you are an idolater, an invoker of devils, you err in faith, speak with temerity, and you have taken an illicit vow."[57]

Jeanne, Daughter of God

The contrast between Jeanne's reaction to the presence of angels and saints in her life and the view that the judges at Rouen took of it opens a perspective on some basic aspects of the way of holiness along which she walked.

Jeanne had been urged by her voices: *Va, fille Dieu, va.* . . . "Go, daughter of God, go. . . ." Yet her mission could not begin until she had pronounced her own *Fiat mihi* . . . "Be it done unto me according to thy word." She had agreed. She left her parents' house and started on the unusual adventure that led her to Chinon, then to Orléans, then to Reims, then to the walls of Paris, to Compiègne where she was captured, and finally to Rouen and the bonfire in which she died. Yet her mission was really fulfilled at the king's coronation. Then indeed, as she confided to Dunois and Regnault de Chartres, Jeanne thought of going home to Domremy;[58] but she had no indication that this was the will of God. The king she had made wished her to remain by his side. He wanted her to be available if needed for further victories, even though his own mind was toying with the possibilities of diplomacy. He was forming the project of detaching Burgundy from England through various concessions, of regaining Paris by compromise rather than through a bloody

---

[57]The remaining articles will be cited in our next chapter.
[58]Dunois: Q, 3:14–15.

assault on the largest and wealthiest city in the kingdom. At this crucial moment Jeanne received no clear guidance from her counsel. She had to decide by herself.

There were several options. Given the reluctance of Charles VII to maintain his armies on a permanent war footing, Jeanne could have teamed up with one of the commanders who could afford to pay his own army. Jean d'Alençon (d. 1476) had little fortune, since most of his lands had been confiscated by the duke of Bedford. Gilles de Rais (1404–1440),[59] though a spendthrift, was still wealthy. At any rate, apart from the period they spent under the spell of Jeanne *la Pucelle*, their careers did not make the idea of the holy kingdom of France too promising. From the standpoint of the knightly ideal that was dear to Jeanne, Dunois and Arthur de Richemont (1393–1458) came out better. But the latter's personal relations with Charles VII were not good.[60] In any case, all such close collaborations would have deprived Jeanne of some of her freedom, and this she could not risk, since her saints could return at any moment to give her new instructions.

As usual, however, Jeanne did not pursue her own wishes. She yielded to the king while maintaining her conviction that peace with the duke of Burgundy would come only "at the tip of the lance." She no doubt had a sense that her mission was done when, after the unsuccessful assault on the walls of Paris between Porte St.-Honoré and Porte St.-Denys (September 8, 1429), she deposited her armor in the church of St. Denys (September 11 or 12) as an homage to this traditional protector of the French monarchy. Yet she did what she could to keep up the offensive, especially when Charles VII agreed to a campaign along the Loire to mop up a few Burgundian places. With Jean d'Alençon she took part in the recovery of St.-Pierre-le-Moûtier (early November), but they failed before La Charité-sur-Loire (November 24), where they gave up the siege of the town after one month.

[59]Also spelled de Retz.

[60]The king's instructions specified that the services of Richemont were not wanted (d'Aulon: Q, 3:98). When he turned up with his army before the battle of Patay, it was Jeanne's common sense that gave him a place in the fighting.

Both major decisions—to continue in active service of the king and to encourage offensive action rather than diplomacy—were her very own, for her voices were now silent on these questions. These decisions were made for the sake of others, namely the king and the kingdom. And Jeanne soon found that they were tearing her in two different directions. Even while he let the army march on Paris, Charles VII was negotiating with the duke of Burgundy. He would not let his weaponry thwart his diplomacy.

During much of the time after the coronation Jeanne was in a quandary. Yet in this quandary she remained totally serene as she pursued what she took to be the necessary aftermath of her essential mission. She still hoped to liberate Paris. She formed the project to free the duke of Orléans from captivity. In a moment of uncertainty as to what to do she might have thought of an expedition against the Hussites of Bohemia.[61] Nothing came of these plans. Rather, since Compiégne was in danger and not far from the capital, there she went. She never gave a thought that it lay in the diocese of Beauvais. Had she known it, it would have meant nothing to her, for she probably was not acquainted with the personality of the bishop of Beauvais, devoted to Isabeau de Bavière, one of the negotiators of the treaty of Troyes, a friend of John of Lancaster. Had she known it, it probably would have made no difference to her determination.

Jeanne was not an ethereal figure lost in dreams. She was very human. It is true that she was undemanding in food, often satisfied with bread dipped in wine, but the bread of her time was more hearty than the one most of us eat. When in the field of action she could remain on horseback for most of the day without food or drink. In prison she never complained of poor or insufficient fare, though she may have suspected the bishop of Beauvais of trying to poison her when she fell sick after eating a dish of fish that he had sent her.[62] Jeanne appreciated the good things of life. She loved horses. When she was asked what kind of horse

[61]The letter to the Hussites of Bohemia, dated March 3, 1530, which exists only in German translation, was originally drawn up in Latin, not in French (Q, 5:156–59). It contains expressions of hostility and vindictiveness that are entirely out of character with Jeanne. For this reason I very much doubt that the letter comes from her at all.

[62]Jean Tiphaine, priest and doctor in medicine: Q, 3:47.

she was riding when she was captured, she specified that it was a *demi-coursier* and added that she had five *coursiers* paid for by the king and at least seven *trottiers*.[63] But she never asked the king for anything "except good weapons, good horses, and money to pay the people of her retinue." Altogether she had ten to twelve thousand *écus,* which, she said, "is not a great treasure to fight a war; it is really little; her brothers must have them now; in any case, what she has is the king's money."

The spiritual senses that allowed her to hear, touch, and even smell the saints of heaven did not empty her normal bodily senses. She liked the feel of beautiful clothes, the fine colorful robes, mantles, and *huques* that were presented to her by the king or by the city of Orléans. But Jeanne was not unduly attached to what she liked. In fact, her fondness for clothes was in part her undoing. For the foot soldier who captured her had only to take hold of the wide sleeve of her *huque* and pull. But Jeanne followed an unwritten rule that she had herself chosen for her behavior in battle. She never used a sword in combat. The hatchet that she sometimes carried in her hand[64] was strictly ornamental. A normal mounted knight assailed by a foot soldier who tried to pull him down would have cut his hand off. But Jeanne remained non-violent to the point of heroism.

It was not what happened to her, good or bad, that mattered. It was that the will of God be done, that she remain faithful to God's call, that she humbly listen to the heavenly voices that guided her, that God dwell in her virgin soul, that she honor the king who holds his kingdom from the king of heaven. And so Jeanne in Rouen did protest being kept in an English prison rather than a church prison; she complained of the promiscuity in which she was forced to live, with enemy soldiers night and day in her cell instead of women guarding her, of being kept in shackles that were fastened to a heavy piece of wood[65] instead of

[63]T, 1:115. A *coursier* or *demi-coursier* was the customary horse for battle; a *trottier* was the horse for traveling long distances.

[64]On June 8, 1429, Guy and André de Laval wrote to their mother and grandmother: "I saw her mount her horse, armored all in white except her head, a small hatchet in her hand, on a big black horse" (Q, 5:107).

[65]That Jeanne was kept in shackles while in her cell, and more so at night, is attested by many witnesses, notably Manchon (Q, 3:140),

being able to move, of being deprived of Mass and Holy Communion. From the time she arrived in Rouen in December 1430 through the length of her trial,[66] a period of more than five months, she was not allowed to receive the Eucharist. Nicolas Loyseleur, the priest who heard her confession in prison, was an impostor who pretended to be a friend. She was not even allowed to stop by the chapel on the way to the tribunal.[67] She did assail the bishop of Beauvais for stealing the ring her brother had given her. She maintained the right to escape. But she never complained of losing all the things she liked. And in spite of the insinuations of her judges and the daily taunts of her guards, she never entertained the notion that the angels, the saints, or God might have abandoned her.

Massieu (155), Pierre Daron (200). The witnesses differ on another point: Manchon affirms that there was no bed or cubicle in her prison cell *(non erat in eodem carcere aliquid lectus seu aliquod cubile)*, but Massieu states the opposite *(et erat ibidem lectus in quo cubabat)*. Of course the bed may not have been there all the time; yet I am inclined to believe Massieu, who had to enter the cell each time he led Jeanne to the sessions, and he also provides the best details: Jeanne was "in a medium-size room to which one went up eight steps *(in quadam camera media in qua ascendebatur per octo gradus)*." All agree that Jeanne was heavily shackled.

[66]Martin Ladvenu was allowed to hear her confession and to take her Holy Communion before her final sentencing and execution on May 30 (Q, 3:168).

[67]Jean Massieu: Q, 3:151.

SIX

Jeanne and the Church

Jeanne *la Pucelle's* relation to the Church has been made ambiguous by the circumstances of her death and the events that followed. On the one hand, there was the tribunal of the "Roman and Universal Inquisition of Heretical Depravity," which on May 29, 1431, found her guilty of a multitude of sins of witchcraft, immorality, lying, heresy, etc., and of relapsing into the deadly sin of heresy, and which as a consequence abandoned her to the secular arm to be burned. On the other hand, there was the special commission appointed by the Holy See, which on July 7, 1456, annulled her condemnation and declared it to have been entirely erroneous and illegitimate. What chiefly prompted the declaration of nullity was that the trial in Rouen was tainted with numberless canonical irregularities and that no evidence of heresy was found in Jeanne's actions as reported by witnesses or in her statements as recorded in the minutes of the trial.

The tribunal headed by Bishop Cauchon contradicted itself at a crucial point. The vote to abandon Jeanne to the secular arm as a relapsed heretic was taken on May 29. Yet having found her guilty of heresy, the bishop allowed her to receive the sacraments on the morning of May 30 before being led to the fire in which she would die. She was given absolution and Holy Communion by Martin Ladvenu, who, despite his manifest kindness to her, had concurred with the bishop's judgment that she was guilty as accused. In this the bishop's attitude was consistent, if on the one hand he felt certain, officially, that he had formally proven his case against Jeanne in the external forum, and if on the other hand he also thought, as a personal but not official opinion, that she was not guilty in the internal forum. In other words, she had done what she was accused of, but her conscience was clear. Duplicity this undoubtedly was on the bishop's part, but it was the duplicity of a fanatical politician who was also a canon lawyer.

The Judgment of Poitiers

In Jeanne's eyes her relation with the Church was quite simple. Just as she was, as her voices declared, "daughter of God," she was also daughter of the Church. The Church nurtured her when she learned her prayers from her mother, Isabelle, when she responded to the bells ringing the Angelus, when she attended Mass and confessed her sins to Guillaume Frontey, the pastor of Domremy. She summed up her attitude on March 17: "I love the Church and I would like to support it with all my power for our Christian faith, and I am not the one who should be waylaid or hindered from going to church or hearing mass."[1] Jeanne knew that her relation to God came entirely from God's initiative and that it was mediated by angels and saints. Into this area of her life she was most reluctant to let anyone look, including priests and bishops: "As to my good works and my mission, I must refer to the King of Heaven, who has sent me to Charles, son of Charles, king of France, and who will also be king of France."[2] *Je m'en rapporte à Dieu . . . ,*[3] "I refer to God . . . , to the King of Heaven . . . , to Christ . . ." are recurrent expressions in her responses. Again, as reported in the minutes, "I refer to Our Lord who has sent me, to Our Lady and to all the blessed saints in Paradise. And it seems to her that it is one and the same, Our Lord and the Church, and that one should not create a difficulty, asking why make a difficulty about being all one."[4] The tribunal chose to see Jeanne's appeals to God as a way

[1] T, 1:165–66.

[2] T, 1:166. A few pages down Jeanne says that "of the love or hatred that God has for the English or what God does to their souls she knows nothing; but she knows well that they will be pushed out of France, excepting those who will die there, and that God will give a great victory to the French against the English" (169–70).

[3] In Latin, *refero me ad Deum;* see above, chapter 5, note 46.

[4] T, 1:166. The Latin text is clearer, but it is biased against Jeanne: *Et videtur mihi quod unum et idem est de Deo et de Ecclesia, et quod de hoc non*

of escape from questions regarding which Church—militant or triumphant—had a right to know the truth. But in reality, "I refer to . . ." expressed the most profound attitude of her soul before God. It was a reliance that was made of faith, trust, and total love.

This was precisely what the array of theologians and canon lawyers who were gathered by the dauphin in Poitiers had perceived. Jeanne testified before them in March and April 1429 concerning her mission. Although what Jeanne called "the book in Poitiers" has disappeared, the conclusions reached by the churchmen have been preserved. The text begins by formulating a double principle. Such a matter must be investigated according to reason and faith, that is, "by human caution, enquiring into her life, behavior, and intention," and "by devout prayer, asking for a sign of some divine work or expectation by which one may judge that she has come by the will of God."[5] The first line of inquiry led to this conclusion: "In her one finds no evil but only good, humility, virginity, devotion, honesty, simplicity." To the second line of inquiry Jeanne responded that the sign was still to come: "She will show it before the city of Orléans and nowhere else, for this is God's command to her." The scholars recommended that the king let her go to Orléans to show this sign, "for to doubt or abandon her without any evidence of evil would be to oppose the Holy Spirit and to become unworthy of God's aid, as Gamaliel said about the apostles in a council of the Jews." This judgment was in harmony with Jeanne's simple Christian life and her desire as to what she considered to be her divine mission.

Jeanne's Flags

Jeanne's understanding of herself, her mission, and her relation to the Church was represented pictorially, for everyone to see, on her standards and flags. Two flags were painted for her

---

debet fieri difficultas. Quare facitis vos de hoc difficultatem? It is doctrinally more accurate to see an identity between Christ (who is Our Lord in his human nature) and the Church than between God and the Church.

[5]Q, 2:391–92.

and according to her instructions by a Scotsman who resided in Tours, Hauves Poulnoir.[6] There was a great standard that she liked to have by her side in battle and that was carried into the cathedral of Reims for the king's coronation. There was a smaller pennon, possibly triangular. And there was in addition a banner for use by the clergy.

It was chiefly Jeanne's great standard that intrigued the judges, presumably because its display in battle had spread fear in the English ranks. Jeanne liked to hold it herself in order not to kill anyone, and as she said, she never did kill anyone.[7] She even assisted fallen enemies who were dying. In Orléans she had called for the standard when she was already mounted, ready to go to the gate and attack the St.-Loup battery; her page Louis de Coutes lowered it to her through a second-floor window.[8] At Orléans on May 7, 1430, it was when the soldiers saw Jeanne's standard, held by a man from the Basque country, waving in front of the wall of Fort Les Tourelles that they rallied and took the fort.[9] Under the walls of Jargeau Jeanne was climbing a ladder with her standard when she was hit by a stone and fell, but the city was stormed as soon as she got up.[10]

For the images to be painted on the flags Jeanne followed her voices' instructions: "It was because the voices told her, 'Take this standard in the name of the King of Heaven,' that she had the image of Our Lord and of two angels done in color, and it was all done by their command."[11] The background was white, strewn with fleurs-de-lys. The fleur-de-lys as symbol of the French monarchy is not a lily even though it may look like one. It represents three white feathers, which in the legend of the conversion of Clovis were brought from heaven by a dove to his wife Clotilde. The feathers stood for the theological virtues of

[6]Identified as Hamish Power by Sackville-West, *Saint Joan of Arc,* 362. According to the records of the royal treasurer, Hauves Poulnoir was paid twenty-five livres tournois for painting the standard and the pennon (Q, 5:258).

[7]T, 1:78.

[8]Q, 3:69.

[9]Q, 3:216–17.

[10]Q, 3:97.

[11]T, 1:173.

faith, hope, and charity, which in Catholic theology are imparted
in baptism. The legend must have been known to Jeanne, since
it was connected with the baptism of Clovis by St. Remi. At the
center of the white field was a painting of Jesus as king of heaven
and earth sitting on a throne between two angels and holding
the sphere of the world in his hand. The judges tried to have
Jeanne identify the angels: Are they Michael and Gabriel? Are
they the angels in charge of watching over the world? And why
are there only two? But Jeanne brought them back to what was
for her the essential point: The angels were there "only for the
honor of Our Lord."[12] The hope of victory was founded neither
on the standard nor on herself: "It was founded on Our Lord
and nowhere else."[13]

When pressed for the reason why the angels were depicted
with "arms, feet, legs, dresses," and asked if this was how she saw
them, she simply replied that they were on the standard "as they
are painted in churches."[14] The light that accompanied the angels when they appeared to her was not painted because she had
no order to show it. The words *Jhesus Maria* were written along
the side, though this was done at the suggestion of the clergy,
not of the Lord. The standard obviously represented the lordship
of Christ over the kingdom of France, which was one of the basic
points of Jeanne's view of politics.

The pennon, a flame, was smaller. The picture on it showed
the annunciation to Mary and included an angel presenting her
with a lily. This, of course, was no longer the royal fleur-de-lys
but the lily of many a Renaissance painting of the annunciation,
a symbol of purity and virginity. Some of the men in her small
retinue, Jeanne reported, had similar pennons made for themselves, and this helped to distinguish them from the other soldiers, but Jeanne did not know if the inscription *Jhesus Maria*
was on these pennons. She never ordered the flags to be blessed
with holy water.[15] Naturally the picture of the annunciation
evoked the incarnation of the Lord, but though Jeanne did not

[12]T, 1:172.
[13]T, 1:173.
[14]T, 1:171.
[15]T, 1:97.

say this, it could also be seen as a tribute to God, who had sent an archangel not only to Mary the Virgin but also to Jeanne *la Pucelle*. In each case the angel brought a mission from the Lord, and Jeanne intended to be faithful to hers, as Mary first of all had been faithful.

As to the banner, it was strictly for use by the clergy. It was not made according to instructions from above or on the clergy's advice but on Jeanne's initiative. Jeanne's chaplain, the Augustinian Jean Pasquerel, was a lector at the Augustinian friary in Tours. According to his own testimony, he met Jeanne's mother at the great pilgrimage of Notre-Dame du Puy, which was also attended by some of Jeanne's companions on the way from Vaucouleurs to Chinon. They had urged the friar to go back to Chinon with them in order to meet Jeanne. As she was already at Tours, where she was lodged in the home of a certain Jean Dupuy, they continued on to that city. After his interview with *la Pucelle* Pasquerel became her chaplain. He remained with her up to the day of her capture, when he was also taken by the Burgundians. Jeanne's two flags were made in Tours. In addition, when the expedition to Orléans was being prepared in Blois, Jeanne told her chaplain, as he reported, to "have a standard made to gather the priests, what in French is called a *bannière*, and on that standard to have a painting of the image of Our Lord crucified. Which I did."[16]

When he testified in 1456, however, Pasquerel confused the picture on Jeanne's standard and that on the pennon, saying that

> she had asked the messengers of her Lord, that is, of God, who appeared to her what she should do; they told her to take her Lord's standard; that was when she had her standard made, on which there was painted the image of our Savior seated for judgement in the clouds of heaven, and there was a painted angel who carried in his hands a *fleur-de-lys* that God was blessing. I arrived in Tours where this standard was being painted.[17]

The image of the crucifix on the banner had a paraliturgical purpose, for twice a day, morning and evening, the clergy and those soldiers who had received absolution met with Jeanne

[16]Q, 3:104.
[17]Q, 3:103.

around it, and "they sang anthems and hymns to St. Mary." On the way to Orléans along the left bank of the Loire the clergy walked ahead of the soldiers with the banner. This was clearly a hanging banner painted on the frontside only, made to be carried in procession.

Taken together, the pictures on Jeanne's flags show three levels of religious awareness, which are focused on the three fundamental mysteries of the Christian faith. With the image of universal kingship on the great standard, the first level points to the essential order of being: Christ as God is king of all, adored by the angels. Since Christ is in his divinity the Son of God, eternal Word of the Father, this is a rendering of the mystery of the Holy Trinity. The second level, indicated by the annunciation on the pennon, is that of the incarnation of the Second Person: The Word takes flesh from the Virgin Mary, and his coming is attended by the archangel Gabriel. The third level, that of Christ crucified painted on the banner, evidently evokes the redemption, the gathering point of repenting sinners.

In the language of images Jeanne has thus depicted the Church in heaven as pure adoration of God, the Church on earth as pure reception of God in the womb of the Virgin Mary, and sinful humanity, gathered in this Church around the cross along with the priests and soldiers, redeemed and repentant. Yet it is the same Church that is on earth and in heaven. The banner leads and carries the prayers of humankind; the pennon announces the coming of the Lord among us; but it is the great standard that brings victory, in an extension of Jeanne's military principle: "In God's name the soldiers will fight, and God will give the victory."[18] Humans struggle along in imperfect faith and love, but God's graceful gift is the total source of their hope.

The Inquisition

The questioners of Jeanne in Rouen had most likely received instructions from Pierre Cauchon to probe her use of symbols, in which he was eager to uncover underlying superstition

---

[18]This was Jeanne's response to Guillaume Aymeri, one of the clergy who interrogated Jeanne in Poitiers, as reported by Seguin Seguin: Q, 3:204.

and hidden magic. Their questions were grounded in a principle of suspicion that distorted their perception of the universe of Jeanne *la Pucelle*. Her great standard with the inscription *Jhesus Maria* was suspicious. Her ring, the one that had been taken by Burgundians, was inscribed with the same invocation and three small crosses. It became evidence for the accusation: what could they mean and what was their use? There were also five crosses on the sword that had been unearthed at the shrine of St.-Catherine-de-Fierbois.[19] Along with the cross that Jeanne sometimes signed instead of her name, and the one that she occasionally placed next to her signature, and the Fairies' Tree in Domremy with the garlands hung on it by children, and the springs that could be credited with healing powers, they constituted a potentially dangerous complex that could be connected with the darkest designs of witchcraft. At least this was hinted during the trial, and it was included in the innumerable crimes of which Jeanne was declared to be guilty. Whether judges and interrogators really believed this sort of nonsense is, of course, another problem.

As a tribunal of the Roman Inquisition, the court in Rouen was indeed an agency of the institutional, hierarchic, militant Church. And the judges did not fail to remind Jeanne that she was being tried in a matter of faith by an ecclesiastical tribunal with full authority to find her innocent or guilty. The trial was justified because of a public rumor

> that this woman, completely forgetting the honesty that is proper to the female sex, breaking all the restraints of shame, oblivious of all feminine decency, by an astonishing and monstrous deformation wore unusual garments proper to the male sex; and furthermore that her presumption went as far as daring to do, to say, and to spread many things that are outside of and against the Catholic faith, and damaging to the same orthodox faith. She was said to have sinned to no small extent in such matters both in our diocese and in many other places in the Kingdom.[20]

This was argued by Pierre Cauchon de Sommièvre in the letter by which he officially inaugurated the proceedings at the

---

[19]T, 1:171. About the crosses, Jeanne said that she knew nothing.
[20]T, 1:1.

opening session of the tribunal. It was not said in this document, however, and Jeanne had no means of knowing, that the apparent smoothness of the legal machine set up by the bishop was hiding a fierce struggle between the University of Paris and himself. It was agreed among the leaders of the English party that Jeanne *la Pucelle* should be tried for heresy against the faith, for that was the only way she could be abandoned to the secular arm by a Church tribunal, and that the proof of her heresy was the witchcraft in which she had evidently ensnared the English soldiery. But it remained to be decided which ecclesiastical tribunal had jurisdiction over the case.

The University of Paris had been the first to claim jurisdiction. It was the chief teacher of doctrine in the kingdom of France. At the time, of course, Paris was in English hands. Those members of the university who opposed the treaty of Troyes had moved to the central parts of the country, which supported the dauphin. The clerics who had examined Jeanne in Poitiers had been chiefly drawn from this group. Their colleagues who had remained in Paris had espoused the cause of Henry VI of England. In November 1430 the university invited Cauchon, politely but firmly, to turn over the prisoner to the ecclesiastical tribunal of Paris, where she would be kept safely in the power of Msgr. the Inquisitor of Heretical Perversity.[21]

Although he had been, in 1403, rector of the University of Paris, the bishop of Beauvais was determined to chair the tribunal himself. Part of the population of Paris was not favorable to the double monarchy. And the others were too much under the influence of the duke of Burgundy, who from the point of view of the duke of Bedford could not be entirely trusted. Philippe *le Bon* had in fact facilitated the task of Jeanne at Orléans by withdrawing his troops from the siege a few days before Jeanne's arrival. The duke of Bedford was therefore determined that the trial would take place in the safer city of Rouen, and he made it clear that should the Church tribunal fail to find Jeanne guilty, she would remain a prisoner in English hands.[22]

[21]Q, 1:15–16.
[22]This was clearly stated in the official letter of Henry VI to Bishop Cauchon: *Toutefois, c'est notre intention de ravoir et reprendre par devers*

Yet the venue of the trial in Rouen had to be carefully negotiated. In France, at least, a heresy trial was a joint affair that involved the diocesan bishop of the territory, either in person or through his delegates, and the Holy See through the officers of the Roman Inquisition, most of whom belonged to the Order of Preachers. The head of the Inquisition for the kingdom of France could easily have traveled from Paris to Rouen to preside with Cauchon. The university would be consulted at the proper time. But Jeanne would be tried in Rouen by a properly constitutioned court of the Inquisition under the authority of himself as bishop. But was he qualified for the function? He based his qualification on the fact that Jeanne had committed some of her alleged crimes in his jurisdiction, in which she had also been captured. Compiègne was indeed in the diocese of Beauvais. Apparently Cauchon did not want to know that Jeanne had been captured on the other side of the river Oise, which was in the diocese of Senlis.

That Pierre Cauchon seldom resided in his diocese was of course irrelevant. Being also *vidame,* or vice-dean, of the canonical chapter of the cathedral of Reims, he spent much time in that city, not far from his family residence at Sommièvre. He had fled from Reims in haste on the arrival of the French army for the coronation of Charles VII. Above all, Pierre Cauchon was a court bishop who liked to operate at the highest levels of the kingdom. He was close to queen Isabeau de Bavière and the duke of Bedford. But he had no jurisdiction in Rouen.

As the see of Rouen happened to be vacant, the duke of Bedford could easily intimidate the canons of the cathedral: On December 28, 1430, the chapter of canons decided that for the duration of the trial the location of the proceedings would be exempt from the jurisdiction of Rouen and transferred to that of Beauvais.[23] Such a transfer was a legal fiction. Whether the chapter had the authority to do it was debatable, since during a vacancy the chapter of canons cannot have more authority than the

---

nous icelle Jeanne, si ainsi était qu'elle ne fut convaincue ou atteinte des cas susdits ou d'aucun d'eux ou d'autre touchant ou regardant notre dite foi (T, 1:15).

[23]T, 1:16–18.

ordinary of the see, and if a bishop can grant jurisdiction, he cannot alienate any part of his territory and place it in another diocese. But this was the nearest that Pierre Cauchon could come to ensure the legality of his presidency of the tribunal. The important point for him was the outcome: if Jeanne was found guilty the tribunal would decide, depending on the gravity of the matter, on a term of prison that could be for life. Were she found to be a relapsed heretic she must be handed over to the secular arm for death by fire. The duke of Bedford was determined to obtain the latter. His friend Bishop Cauchon could be trusted to use suitable canonical forms to ensure that the regent of France was not disappointed. Jeanne would be found guilty to the fullest extent, and she would be burned at the stake.

To bring this about and to offer the English lords what he called "a beautiful trial,"[24] Cauchon aligned an impressive list of judges and no less impressive a list of assessors and lawyers who functioned as interrogators of Jeanne and as advisers to the judges. There was no legal defender for the accused. It is probably not irrelevant that Bishop Cauchon had good relations with the Bishop of Rome, who was duly informed of the condemnation of Jeanne. Yet Martin V may have had doubts about Pierre Cauchon. In spite of being presented by the king of England and recommended by the University of Paris, Cauchon was not promoted to the archdiocese of Rouen when his diocese of Beauvais definitely returned into French hands. In 1432 Eugene IV transferred Cauchon to the see of Lisieux, still in English-held Normandy. This was done in part for political reasons, since Cauchon would not return to Beauvais; it was by no means a promotion. The bishop died at Lisieux in wealth and honors in 1442.

Jeanne's View of the Clergy

This is a suitable point to reflect on the discrepancy between Jeanne's view of the clergy and the actual role of priests in the society of her times. On the one side we see a young woman

---

[24]Manchon: "The bishop told him that it was proper to serve the king and that they intended to make a beautiful trial against the said Jeanne" (Q, 3:137).

who is eager to "cleanse her conscience" and prepared to confess her sins to all the priests she meets. She has confessed her sins to the pastor of Vaucouleurs and is shocked when the priest throws holy water at her at the request of Baudricourt. She is assiduous at confession to Pasquerel, but she also confesses her sins to Brother Richard, although he also came at her with holy water. She even asks Bishop Cauchon to hear her in the sacrament of penance. The priests who accompany the army to Orléans she orders to march in procession and sing hymns. She wants them to be available for cleansing the souls of the soldiers and to lead them everyday in evening prayers. She reports to the tribunal that the learned clergy in Poitiers acknowledged her God-given mission "by their science and because they were priests." Yet she had told these clergymen that "there are more things in the books of Our Lord than in theirs." This, I would think, denotes a conception of the priest as being essentially a leader in the spiritual life who adjusts pastoral methods to the ways and levels of the people: chants and processions are proper at the folk level, while research in the books of our Lord should be pursued at a deeper intellectual level. And the "books of Our Lord" were clearly defined in the Augustinian-Franciscan tradition. They were the three books, *natura, Scriptura, anima:* nature, the Scriptures, and the soul. The book of the soul could be explored through a mystical identification of *anima, Maria, Ecclesia,* the soul, the Virgin Mary, the Church. What was believed of the Church as the Bride of Christ and manifest at a high degree in the image of the Mother of God could be experienced in the depths of one's soul. The personal-individual was in harmony with the corporate-ecclesial and exemplified in the special and unique. Although Jeanne could not have formulated it in a formal theological way, this was the horizon in which she lived and thought. The cleansing of conscience rested on the conviction of the holiness of the Church and had a heavenly model in the Mother of God.

By contrast, the books of the clergy, in Poitiers as in Rouen, were the collections of the decrees and decretals of canon law. Like all her contemporaries, Jeanne could not think of a separation between Church and state. The kingdom she fought for was at the same time the kingdom of God and "the holy kingdom of

France," the latter because of the former. The dynastic struggle that provoked the Hundred Years' War was also a struggle within the clergy. On the side of Henry VI and the duke of Bedford, the chancellor of France—a kind of prime minister—was the bishop of Thérouanne and future cardinal Louis de Luxembourg, Cardinal Henry Beaufort (d. 1447), bishop of Winchester, being Henry VI's chancellor for the British Isles. On the side of Charles VII it was the archbishop of Reims, Regnault de Chartres, who was chancellor of the kingdom. Thus the struggle pitted king against king, bishop against bishop, priests against priests. To the collections of canon law, such bishops added the laws of the kingdom and the will of the king or his regent as part of their own book.

An Impressive Array of Judges

When looked at in all its details, the trial of Jeanne precisely takes the sharp colors of a struggle within the Church. Remotely, the struggle is between the partisans of Henry VI and those of Charles VII. Immediately, it is between clerical power and lay powerlessness, between male arrogance and female patience. On the side of sheer power one sees the bishop of Beauvais and his learned clerics. These include a high number of Benedictine abbots (of Fécamp, Cormeilles, Ste-Catherine de Rouen, Jumièges, le Bec-Helluin, Mont-St.-Michel,[25] St.-Corneille de Compiègne), the Cistercian abbot of Mortemer, doctors in theology, doctors in canon law, doctors in both laws, canons, diocesan priests, members of the Benedictine, Dominican, Franciscan, Augustinian, and Carmelite Orders.[26] Several bishops appeared toward the end of the proceedings, notably some from Normandy: Philibert de Montjeu (d. 1439) of Coutances and the Italian Zanon de Castiglione (d. 1459) of Lisieux, both taking part in the deliberations of Easter Week when the seventy articles of

[25]Though the fortress and abbey of Mont-St-Michel were never conquered by the partisans of Henry VI, Abbot Robert Jolivet (d. 1444) abandoned his abbey in 1419 to join the cause of the double monarchy; he took up residence in Rouen.

[26]I take these and the following details from T, 2:383–425.

accusation were condensed into twelve, and Jean de Mailly (d. 1477) of Noyon. Louis de Luxembourg was in attendance on May 23, and he was again present in the St. Ouen cemetery and at the Old Market Place. From England there were a few priests, along with William Alnwick (d. 1449), bishop of Norwich, and the English cardinal Henry Beaufort, archbishop of Winchester, chancellor of England and great uncle of Henry VI, both of whom watched the chaotic proceedings of May 24 in the cemetery of St. Ouen.

On the other side, facing them, the lone figure of Jeanne, "about nineteen years old," as she said, kept in chains in an English prison. A conjunction of sheer brute force and ecclesiastical scholarship stands over against a young woman who has readily admitted to the learned clerics of Poitiers, "I know neither *A* nor *B*,"[27] of whom her hostess at Bourges, Marguerite La Touroulde, was to declare: "Jeanne was very simple and ignorant, and she knew absolutely nothing, it seems to me, except in the matter of war."[28] Yet, still according to La Touroulde, this Jeanne had declared to the learned clerics who had tested her at Poitiers, "There are more things in Our Lord's books than in yours."[29]

Dissent Among the Judges

It would nonetheless be too simplistic to see the institutional Church as such pitched against Jeanne in this unequal battle. In Rouen itself the officers of the Church were not of one mind. Cauchon ran into difficulties precisely with the institutions when he set up his array of judges. The Dominican Jean Graverent, Great Inquisitor for France since 1424, did not go to Rouen as he was busy farther out, in Coutances, on another case. His assistant for the diocese of Rouen, vice-inquisitor Jean Le Maistre, O.P., did not wish to be involved. From January 9 when the proceedings started to February 19 he stayed away. Then he began to attend without taking part. Only when he received extended faculties from Graverent on March 12 did he consent to

[27]Gobert Thibault: Q, 3:74.
[28]Q, 3:87.
[29]Q, 3:86.

co-preside the tribunal. But he does not seem to have ever initiated anything beyond asking some of the questions.

Certainly Jeanne had determined opponents among the judges and assessors. Three are mentioned by Guillaume Manchon: Jean Beaupère, Nicolas Midi, and Jacques de Touraine.[30] Others, however, were just as hostile. Beside the bishop of Beauvais there were Jean d'Estivet, promoter of the faith in the diocese of Beauvais, who frequently insulted Jeanne; the abbot of Fécamp; and several theologians who had come from the Sorbonne, notably Thomas de Courcelles, one of the three who voted that Jeanne be tortured. The two others who voted for torture on May 12 were Raoul Morel, a canon lawyer in Rouen, and Nicolas Loyseleur, a canon of Rouen, born near Chartres.[31] The case of Loyseleur deserves some comment, since several statements that were made in the nullity investigation point to him as Jeanne's worst enemy besides the duke of Bedford and the bishop of Beauvais. With Cauchon's authorization this priest disguised himself as a layman, faked being a Lorrainer, and befriended Jeanne in her prison. What reason he may have given her for being able to enter her cell we do not know. During one of his conversations with her Manchon and Guillaume Colles were hidden in the next room, from which they could see and hear Jeanne, but they refused to record it: "I answered that I must not do so, that it was dishonest to begin the trial with that kind of hoax." After a while he revealed to her that he was a priest and he heard her confession several times. He generally advised her not to trust the judges and to listen only to himself. It seems likely that he reported to the bishop what he could learn from her confessions.[32] That Jeanne's voices gave her no lights on this impostor contributed to her ordeal, and she must have had too high a regard for the priesthood to suspect evil in his doings.

Others among judges and assessors attended the trial more or less under duress. Richard de Grouchet affirmed that he himself

[30]Q, 3:140.

[31]Morel declared that torture would bring out "the truth about her lies"; Loyseleur opined that it would be "a medicine for her soul" (T, 1:351).

[32]Q, 3:141.

and also Jean Pigache and Pierre Minier were forced to give their opinion and to take part in the trial "under threats and in great terror."[33] Yet some of the learned scholars who were invited by the bishop of Beauvais to participate in what modern journalists would call the "trial of the century" refused to do so. A canon lawyer, Jean Lohier, who was passing through Rouen while the trial was underway, was asked for his opinion. According to Thomas de Courcelles, Lohier declared that "it seems to him that one should not proceed against Jeanne in a matter of faith without previously obtaining information on her reputation, and that such information was required by law."[34] The chief secretary of the tribunal, who was responsible for taking the minutes of the proceedings, Guillaume Manchon, provided more elaborate information: Lohier asked for two or three days of reflection before giving his opinion, but Cauchon insisted on an immediate reaction. Lohier's judgment was then given: the proceedings are null for many reasons. The trial is not carried out, as it should be, in a purely ecclesiastical court, and thus the liberty of the participants is not guaranteed; it deals with matters that touch the honor of the king of France, and therefore the king should be heard; the accused was not notified beforehand of any of the accusations, as she should have been, and although she is a very simple person she is deprived of counsel's assistance. Manchon went on to report that Cauchon gathered his chief associates on a Saturday afternoon in Lent and informed them that he would disregard Lohier's views. On the following Sunday, Lohier told Manchon: "You see how they proceed. They will catch her if possible in her own words, that is, when she says, 'I know for certain' concerning her apparitions; but if she said, 'It seems to me,' instead of 'I know for certain,' it is my opinion that no man could condemn her. It seems that they proceed more with hatred than otherwise, and for this reason I will not stay for I do not want to be there."[35]

---

[33]Grouchet: Q, 2:356–57.

[34]Courcelles: Q, 3:58; Machon: Q, 3:138.

[35]Royal inquiry of 1450: Q, 2:11–12; these points are repeated in Q, 3:137–38.

Nicolas de Houppeville participated in some of the preliminary deliberations when he objected that neither the bishop nor the judges had any authority in a case that had already been adjudicated by a tribunal in Poitiers under the authority of the very metropolitan of the bishop of Beauvais, the archbishop of Reims. He further denied that the bishop of Beauvais had any authority on himself, a priest of the diocese of Rouen. Houppeville was then arrested by English soldiers and he spent some time in prison "at the request of the bishop of Beauvais." It was, he reported, through the pressing intervention of Gilles de Duremort, abbot of the Holy Trinity in Fécamp, that he was released from jail.[36]

Among those who took an active part in the trial, a few did object to some aspects of the proceedings. André Marguerie, a canon of Rouen, thought it was an irregularity to keep her in an English prison, but he does not seem to have protested.[37] On one occasion Jean de Châtillon, having suggested that Jeanne was not bound to answer a question on the state of her soul, was sharply told by Pierre Cauchon to shut up and let the judges speak.[38] According to Richard de Grouchet, the few who tried to help Jeanne were "harshly and sharply rebuked, and suspected of partiality, sometimes by the bishop Beauvais in person, sometimes by Master Jean Beaupère, who told them to let her talk, that he was in charge of the questioning."[39] Another, Pierre Minier, encouraged her "after the first sermon," and as a result he thought himself in great danger. This may have been after the charitable exhortation of April 18 when Jeanne was sick, although Minier is not listed among those who accompanied Bishop Cauchon to her cell, or else on May 24 after the solemn sermon in the cemetery of St.-Ouen and her "abjuration." As secretary Manchon remembered on May 12, 1456, there were a

[36]Nicolas de Houppeville gave his own devastating testimony at the nullity inquiry: Q, 3:171–73. Moreover, the Dominican Pierre Bosquier was taken to prison when, shortly after the trial, he denied in public that justice had been done.

[37]Q, 3:184.

[38]Q, 3:153. See below, note 41.

[39]Q, 3:129–30.

few who on occasion tried to advise Jeanne,[40] notably the Dominicans Isambart de la Pierre and Martin Ladvenu but also Jean de Châtillon[41] and Jean de la Fontaine.

More damaging to the validity of the trial and the integrity of Bishop Cauchon is the case of Jean de la Fontaine. In the minutes of the first public audience on February 2, 1431, this canon lawyer is mentioned just after the bishop of Beauvais and Jean d'Estivet. He is given the titles of "counselor, commissary, and examinator of the trial." Jean de la Fontaine was sufficiently trusted by the bishop to question Jeanne in his absence. Until March 17 he was in fact a frequent interrogator of Jeanne. He led the group of those who went to her cell on March 17, the eve of Passion Sunday. Then Jean de la Fontaine is never again mentioned in the minutes. On Palm Sunday it was the main group of Jeanne's enemies—Cauchon, Midy, Beaupère, Maurice, Courcelles—that visited her and exhorted her to abandon her male dress and take up the garments that were proper to her sex. At the beginning of Holy Week Jeanne asked to be allowed to attend Mass, and she repeated that "changing her dress is not in her power . . . , that this dress does not change her soul, and that wearing it is not against the Church!"[42]

That Jean de la Fontaine had a substantial disagreement with Cauchon is clear from secretary Manchon's testimony: Jean de la Fontaine fled from Rouen in haste after making an unauthorized visit to Jeanne, along with Isambart and Ladvenu, during Holy Week, and he never came back.[43] It was precisely during Holy Week that a list of seventy counts of accusation was finalized under the direction of d'Estivet. The list was read to Jeanne

[40]Q, 3:139.

[41]Jean Massieu reported that Châtillon attended the trial as assessor until he privately expressed the view that the proceedings were legally null and void; from then on he was not convoked to the sessions and he no longer attended (Q, 3:153). Yet Massieu must have had the wrong person in mind, for Jean de Châtillon was present in the torture chamber on May 9 (T, 1:348), attended the formal condemnation (T, 1:375), and agreed that Jeanne had relapsed and must be handed over to the secular arm (T, 1:400).

[42]T, 1:183.

[43]Manchon: Q, 3:311.

on Easter Tuesday, March 27, when she denied the truth of most
of them. If Jean de la Fontaine went to Jeanne during Holy
Week, it could only have been to warn her of what was coming
and to try to ward it off by immediately changing to female
dress. He had presumably ordered the English guards out of her
cell, and these must have reported it to the count of Warwick,
governor of the castle. La Fontaine and the bishop must have
had a heated exchange, and the commissary fled to safety.

As to Isambart de la Pierre and Martin Ladvenu, it is in-
conceivable that they were not also threatened by Cauchon. Yet
they remained in Rouen and kept their functions in the trial. One
may presume that as Dominicans stationed at the house of the
Friars Preachers in Rouen they were not free to go. But given the
bishop's determination not to be thwarted in his Machiavellian
plan for the prisoner, it is most probable that in exchange for
their safety they made a promise to him, a promise that Jean de
la Fontaine would not make. In fact, Richard de Grouchet,
Jean Pigache, Jean de Châtillon, Isambart de la Pierre, Martin
Ladvenu—all of them presented as having reservations about the
trial—are listed among the assessors who on May 29 agreed that
Jeanne had relapsed into her errors and should be handed over
to the secular arm for burning. They must have promised to support the conclusions of the majority, thus ensuring the unanimity of the condemnation of Jeanne. On that day Jeanne had only
enemies in the array of lawyers who presumed to judge her. By
that time Jean de la Fontaine was out of reach. He must have dis-
agreed with the substance of the accusations, and he could not
in conscience promise to abide by the decision of the judges.

Warnings to the Bishop

Clearly *la Pucelle* knew nothing of whatever was happening
behind the scenes or of the bishop of Beauvais' maneuvers. But
she could easily see that Cauchon was not impartial. She did
protest against being kept in an English prison, against the conditions of her imprisonment, against taking a new oath to tell the
truth at the start of each session, against the constant jumping
from one topic to another in her questioning, against bringing in
matters that had nothing to do with the question of whether she

was a witch and a heretic, against being deprived of the sacraments, and against harping back on points that were settled in
Poitiers. On February 22 Jeanne warned everyone in general: "If
you were properly informed about me you would wish me out of
your hands. I have done nothing except by revelation."[44] Several
times she warned the bishop of Beauvais in particular to be careful not to judge unjustly. On February 24 she told the questioner: "It may be that about many things you could ask me I
will not tell you the truth, especially in regard to the revelations;
for you could perchance force me to say something that I have
sworn not to say. Thus I would perjure myself, a thing that you
should not wish." Then she turned to Bishop Cauchon: "Think
that you say you are my judge, for you assume a heavy charge
and you charge me too much."[45] She repeated the warning some
minutes later: "You say that you are my judge; be careful what
you do; for indeed I have been sent by God, and you place yourself in great danger."[46] And she also addressed the bishop of
Beauvais to say that "the voices told her many things to report
to the king, not to him."[47] Three weeks later, Jeanne was asked
what this great danger could be. She repeated: "What it was and
is, is what I say to Monsignor of Beauvais: You say that you are
my judge; I do not know if you are, but be careful not to judge
wrongly, for you would put yourself in great danger; and I warn
you, so that if Our Lord punishes you for it, I do my duty by
telling you."[48]

Who Is the True Pope?

One of the questions that was thrown at Jeanne concerned
her judgment on the specific problem of the time regarding the
papacy: which one is the true pope? At the beginning of the session of March 1 the questioner suddenly asked what she thinks
of our lord the pope, and which one she believes is the true

[44]T, 1:46. The Latin text has: *vos deberetis velle,* "you should wish."
[45]T, 1:55.
[46]T, 1:59.
[47]T, 1:60.
[48]T, 1:147–48.

one.[49] Her response was that of one who does not know that there is a schism within the Catholic Church, for she asked, "Are there two [popes]?"

In spite of the largely successful efforts of the Council of Basle, there were still more than one person who claimed to be the Bishop of Rome, so that the Christian world was divided in the papacy itself. The interrogator in fact knew more than he had let out, for he confronted Jeanne with a copy of a letter she had sent on the matter to the comte d'Armagnac. He also had a copy of the count's letter to her. Jean IV, comte d'Armagnac, had sent a messenger to Jeanne, for he wished to know from her "to which of the three Supreme Pontiffs he ought to give his obedience."[50] This was in August 1429, during Jeanne's first stay in Compiègne. In fact, the count's request was quite detailed: should we follow Martin V, who was elected during the Council of Constance and is in Rome, or Clement VIII, who was elected to succeed Benedict XIII by a few cardinals at Paniscole in the province of Valencia in Spain, where he still is, or Benedict XIV, who was elected by only one cardinal to succeed Benedict XIII and whose whereabouts are unknown to the count? Jeanne had dictated a short answer: she was too busy with matters of war to respond now; but he should send her another messenger when he hears that she is in Paris. By that time she would have received her counsel's advice and she would respond properly.

Jeanne's memory being triggered by the reading of the two letters, she recognized that she had received the count's messenger just when she was about to mount her horse. The letter that was read was, she said, in part correct, but not entirely. She had answered briefly "among other things that she would give a proper answer from Paris or from somewhere else when she has peace." But she had received no revelation about the question and she did not know which pontiff God wanted the count to acknowledge. She thought nonetheless that we should give obedience to "our pope who is in Rome." She also told the messenger several things that were not written in her letter to the count,

[49]T, 1:81.

[50]The two letters are contained in articles 26–30 in the seventy articles of accusation, March 27 (T, 1:224–26).

and it was about these that she intended to write later at greater length. However, the count's messenger seems to have been more insistent for an immediate answer than Jeanne's companions were inclined to tolerate, for she added, "If he had not withdrawn fast he could have been thrown into the water, though not by herself."[51]

One can throw some light on this incident. Jean IV d'Armagnac (1418–1450) had succeeded his father, Bernard VII (1391–1418), a victim of the massacre that on June 12, 1418, followed the entrance of the duke of Burgundy, Jean *Sans-peur,* into the city of Paris. The Armagnac party carried his family's name, and he was himself a determined supporter of Charles VII. After the Council of Pisa (1414) and the division of Christendom in three papal obediences, the county of Armagnac had remained faithful to the last of the Avignon popes, Benedict XIII, and it had later recognized his successor Clement VIII. It was precisely in 1428 that Jean d'Armagnac switched ecclesial allegiance and aligned himself with Charles VII in favor of Martin V, who was by then the pope in Rome. The count must have sent his message to *la Pucelle* in the hope of obtaining supernatural advice. But in this case he made the same mistake as Charles II of Lorraine when Jeanne had her audience at the ducal palace in Nancy: they both assumed that she had or could obtain information on questions that were of concern to themselves. With Charles it was his health. With Jean it was his ecclesial obedience. But Jeanne claimed no privileged knowledge of anything outside her mission. Simply, she followed the pope who was in Rome. This was Martin V. Yet it is possible that she did not even know his name, since she did not give it.

When Jeanne responded in prison with the query, "Are there two [popes]?"[52] she may well have believed that the matter of the double or triple papacy was settled. In fact, when she was a child in Domremy and both France and England supported John XXIII (pope, 1410–1415), the bishoprics of Lorraine were in the obedience of Benedict XIII, along with Scotland and most of Spain. It was this pope who had been approached for the bull

[51]T, 1:224.
[52]T, 1:81.

of confirmation of Philippe de Ville-sur-Illon as bishop of Toul in 1401, and again, when Philippe died, for the confirmation of his cousin Henri de Ville in 1408. Henri, who remained in the see of Toul till he died in 1430, was Jeanne's bishop.[53] Yet with most German princes the metropolitan for Lorraine, the archbishop and Great Elector of Trèves,[54] had opted for Gregory XII (pope, 1406–1415). By 1429–1430, however, the bishops of Lorraine were following Martin V (1417–1431), around whom most of the Christian world was rallying.

How much of this Jeanne knew cannot be ascertained. She was neither a diplomat nor a canon lawyer. What she stated was the principle, it is the Bishop of Rome who is, as was still said in certain ecclesiastical circles, "vicar of God" on earth.[55]

This simple principle stands against the contention of the tribunal that Jeanne is "evil-thinking in regard to our Catholic faith, schismatic, dubious and devious on the article *Unam sanctam* and several other articles of this same faith."[56] In keeping with the normal procedure Jeanne should have responded to each article of accusation with *Credo* or *Non credo,* that is, "aye" (guilty, the article is correct) or "nay" (not guilty, the article is not correct), refusal to say anything being tantamount to "guilty," as was explained in the presentation of the articles made on March 27. In practice, however, Jeanne was allowed to say more than *credo, non credo.*[57] On a number of articles she said, "I have already answered," or she referred to her previous responses to similar points. The article *Unam sanctam* designated the phrase of the creed, *et unam, sanctam, catholicam et apostolicam ecclesiam.* It was taken by the lawyers to imply the whole structure of the Church militant, including its relation to the Church

[53]Pius Bonifacius Gams, *Series episcoporum ecclesiae catholicae* (Graz: Akademische Verlag, 1957) 636.

[54]From 1418 to 1430 the archbishop of Trèves was Otto, de Ziegenhain; he was followed by Rhaban, de Helmstadt, in 1430 (Gams, *Series,* 318),

[55]The title *vicarius Dei,* used by Innocent III (1198–1216), was favored by papalist canon lawyers; it replaced the older formula, *vicarius Petri.*

[56]T, 1:192.

[57]As explained by Jean d'Estivet at the introduction of the ordinary trial on March 27: T, 1:186.

triumphant. Moreover, in a legal context the words *Unam sanc-tam* could easily evoke the bull *Unam sanctam* of Boniface VIII (November 13, 1302), in which it was solemnly "declared, stated, and defined, that submission to the Roman Pontiff is nec-essary to salvation for every human creature."[58] Now, the most frequent medieval heresy flourished in small sects that tended to identify spiritual experience and mystical perfection, and conse-quently to reject any interference by institutional authority in the life of the perfect.[59] While the tribunal never accused Jeanne of belonging to such a sect, it ascribed to individual sectarianism her repeated assertions that her mission came from God, that she received divine counseling, and that the actions she performed in obedience to her voices were not subject to human judgment. At the heart of Jeanne's views, however, there was again the straightforward principle, "It is one and the same, Our Lord and the Church, and one should not create a difficulty; why do you make a difficulty about being all one?"[60]

Jeanne's unsophisticated yet traditional view of the Church's hierarchic structure is manifest in the appeals to higher authority that she made in the course of her trial. Several times she asked to be sent to the pope of Rome, an appeal that should have halted the proceedings, but that was regularly ignored or dismissed as impractical. Thus on March 17, in answer to the question whether "she thought she would be bound to tell the full truth to the pope, vicar of God, concerning all that she would be asked concerning faith and her conscience," Jeanne "demanded to be sent to him, then she will answer before him all that she must answer."[61] Again, on May 2, following Jean de Châtillon's address on six points, Jeanne was asked if she was willing to submit to our holy father the pope. She responded: "Take me to him, and I will answer him."[62] The appeal was ig-

[58]See my essay "The bull Unam sanctam of Boniface VIII," *Papal Pri-macy and the Universal Church: Lutherans and Catholics in Dialogue, V,* ed. Paul Empie and Austin Murphy (Minneapolis: Augsburg, 1974) 105–19.
[59]Ronald Knox, *Enthusiasm* (Oxford: Clarendon Press, 1950) chs. 5 and 6.
[60]T, 1:166.
[61]T, 1:176.
[62]T, 1:343. One can argue that the judges did not see these words as

nored. Yet Jeanne never blamed the Church for what bishops and priests were doing in its name.

Bishop Cauchon's Evolving Plan

It actually took some time before the bishop of Beauvais found a way that could bring Jeanne to express false doctrine in regard to the Church. The point on which he had originally thought that Jeanne would be found guilty was witchcraft. From the beginning of the interrogations on February 21, until March 17, the questions that came to her in quick succession concerned chiefly her voices, the Fairies' Tree, her sword, her standards, her rings, her horses, the sign of the crown, the shape of angels and saints, her unnatural male dress. In between, questions were thrown in about mortal sins, the assurance of grace, the execution of Franquet,[63] the stealing of a horse from the bishop of Senlis,[64] waging war on certain holy days, leaping from a window at the castle of Beaurevoir. Jeanne, however, had successfully dodged all the snares that had been set to catch her.

Then, on March 15, the prosecution introduced a new principle: "If it has happened that she has done anything that is against our faith, she ought to refer to the determination of Holy Mother Church, to which she must refer."[65] Two days later a new type of question appeared: Jeanne was asked if she was willing "to

---

formal appeals to the Bishop of Rome. Yet the disregard of her request to be judged by the pope was a cause of nullity.

[63]Franquet d'Arras was on trial before the *bailli* of Senlis for being "a murderer, a thief, and a traitor" (T, 1:151). Jeanne persuaded his judges that he should be exchanged for an Armagnac prisoner, "the owner of the Hotel de l'Ours" in Paris. But she added: "When I heard that this man had died, I said to the *bailli:* Since my man is dead, do what you like with the other in keeping with justice."

[64]The horse, Jeanne responded, was not stolen and the bishop was promised payment. The horse was entrusted to La Trémoille, who should have returned it to the bishop, "because I heard that the bishop was angry that the horse was gone, and because it was not good for war" (T, 1:151–52). Jeanne did not think it had been returned and did not know if it was paid for.

[65]T, 1:154.

entrust all she has said and done to the determination of our Mother the Holy Church."[66] The question was repeated: "In regard to what you have said and done, do you refer to the Church's determination?"[67]

Will Jeanne abandon her defense and submit to the Church? There were two sides to the question. First, implicit in it was an identification of the present assembly of judges and assessors with the Church gathered in council. Second, to the men of the tribunal submission to the Church meant donning female dress, going back to the rank of an ignorant lay person, letting the learned clergymen determine the truth or falsity of her voices, and gladly accepting their sentence.

But Jeanne knew that the Church is not where bishops and priests are gathered to punish the innocent. Nothing they did or threatened to do could change her fundamental fidelity. Jeanne even responded to the above question by confessing her love for the Church: "I love the Church and I would like to support it with all my power for the sake of our Christian faith. . . . It seems to me that it is all one, Our Lord and the Church; there is no difficulty. Why is it that you create difficulties?"[68] In turn, the judge followed the new line of the prosecution. He explained "that there is the Church Triumphant, where God, the saints, the angels, and the souls that have been saved are; there is also the Church Militant, in which are the pope, vicar of God on earth, the cardinals, the prelates of the Church, the clergy, and all good Christians and Catholics; and this Church, when properly gathered, cannot err and is governed by the Holy Spirit."[69] Will she then refer to the Church Militant, that which is on earth? The "official procedure" ended on this note.

On Palm Sunday Cauchon and a few others visited the prison to urge Jeanne to take up women's clothes. They met with the refusal that they expected. It was now on the question of clothing that they would hang the judgment that Jeanne was an obstinate heretic. When she insisted that dressing in men's

[66]T, 1:165.
[67]T, 1:166.
[68]T, 1:165.
[69]T, 1:166–67.

clothes was a necessity of her condition, she was, in the judges' mind, contradicting the natural law and the accepted doctrines of the Church on the proper dress of women. That women should not dress like men was taken to be part of true doctrine by virtue of what would be called today "the ordinary magisterium of bishops."

The Ordinary Procedure

The "ordinary procedure" opened on Monday in Holy Week, March 26, in the bishop's chambers. The day after, Cauchon offered Jeanne the advice, if she wished, of some of the learned canon lawyers who were following the trial. She politely thanked him: "First, for your admonition regarding my welfare and our faith I am grateful to you and also to all here present. As to the counsel you offer me, I am also grateful to you; but I have no intention to part with God's counsel."[70]

Jeanne was thus seen to reject the Church's offer of assistance. It was by now clear to the judges that Jeanne would continue to reject any human advice and to abide by her voices and counsel. In this context they could easily find her subversive of the Church of God. The point of this subversion would be her male garments. Jeanne would be caught between two views of the Church, triumphant in heaven and militant on earth. It would be all the easier to find her guilty as such a theological distinction was new to her. That this might not be entirely fair to the accused cannot have escaped some of the judges and assessors. But the inquisitors, who were generally eager to identify heretics, were not overanxious about mistakenly sending the innocent to the fire, for it was generally taught that if such an error was made the victim's soul would be taken straight to heaven.[71]

When pressed on the Church militant, Jeanne had already said on March 17 that she "was sent to the king of France by God, the Virgin Mary, and all the blessed saints of paradise of the victorious Church from above, and by their command, and that to that Church she submits all her good actions and all she has

[70]T, 1:190.
[71]See my book *Satan* (Paris: Desclée, 1988) 129–32.

said and done. And as for answering whether she submits to the Church militant, she will answer no more for the time being."[72] For Jeanne this evidently meant that she needed advice from her voices. To the judges' ears it indicated that she persisted in her refusal to submit to them as spokesmen for the Church. Whether so intended or not, this was the attitude of a heretic.

A few days later, therefore, on Tuesday and Wednesday in Holy Week, March 27 and 28, the seventy points of the accusation were read to the prisoner, who had an opportunity to respond to them. The intent of the document is heavily underlined in the introductory foreword, which is addressed to the bishop of Beauvais and the vice-inquisitor of heretical perversity as "competent judges":

> . . . so that a certain woman commonly called Jeanne. . . be by you. . . sentenced and declared to be a witch or sorceress, a diviner, a pseudo-prophetess, an invocator and conjuror of evil spirits, superstitious, a committed and persistent practitioner of the arts of magic,[73] evil-thinking in regard to our Catholic faith, schismatic, dubious and devious in and on the article *Unam sanctam* etc. and other articles of this faith, sacrilegious, idolatrous, apostate from the faith, evil-speaking and evil-doing, blaspheming God and his saints, scandalous, seditious, a destroyer and spoiler of peace, a warmonger, cruelly thirsting for human blood and encouraging [others] to spill it, utterly shameless in abandoning the decency and congruity of her sex, irreverentiously assuming unnatural dress and the condition of men-at-arms, abominable to God and men in these and other matters, a traitor to divine and natural laws and ecclesiastical discipline, a seductress of princes and people, accepting veneration and adoration in disregard and contempt of God, exhibiting her hands and garments to be kissed, usurping divine honors and cult, heretical or at least strongly suspect of heresy,—and that on all these matters she be canonically and legally punished and corrected according to the divine and canonical determinations. . . .[74]

Jeanne's denial of the competency of the tribunal was exactly what Cauchon expected: "I firmly believe that our holy

[72]T, 1:167.
[73]The Latin has *magicis artibus implicita ac insistens.*
[74]T, 1:192.

father the Roman pope, the bishops and other ecclesiastical men must preserve the Catholic faith and punish those who fall. But as to me I submit my actions only to the heavenly Church, that is, to God, the Virgin Mary, and the saints of Paradise. And I firmly believe that I have not failed in our Christian faith and I would not wish to fail."[75] Jeanne nonetheless spoke to the other articles. All in all, she denied that they were true, and she expressed her entire reliance on Our Lord.

Jeanne was questioned again in her prison on Holy Saturday, when she was asked if she was willing to refer to "the judgment of the Church on earth for all she had said and done, whether in good or in evil, especially in regard to the causes, crimes, and delicts of which she is accused and to all that touches her trial."[76] By this question Jeanne was enjoined to agree beforehand to whatever the tribunal would decide. Her fate would be decided by what she said about the Church militant. She was asked specifically if she would refer to the Church militant should this Church tell her that "her revelations are illusions, diabolical phenomena, superstitions, or evil things."

At this point Jeanne's answer was twofold. On the one hand, she "will refer to the Church Militant, provided she is not asked for something impossible." On the other hand, she "will trust Our Lord, whose command she will always fulfil; and she knows well that what is contained in the trial happened by the command of God; and as to what she has affirmed in the trial having been done by the command of God, it would be impossible for her to do the opposite. And in case the Church Militant order her to do the opposite, she will refer to no one in the world except to God, and she will always do the good precept of God himself."[77] On Easter Monday, April 2, the judges drew their conclusion: Jeanne will be subjected to "charitable exhortations," the usual preliminaries to the tribunal's ultimate deliberations and sentencing.

The timing of this central part of the trial is really incredible. Did it ever occur to the bishop and his assistants that all this

[75]T, 1:193.
[76]T, 1:287.
[77]T, 1:287–88.

was taking place in Holy Week? Devoted to her Lord Jesus Christ as *la Pucelle* was, should not Holy Week have been expected to bring her new light on the passion she was going through? Surely it did not augur well for the bishop's case that Jeanne could find comfort in sharing the agony of her Lord. The final act of the office proceedings—the exhortation to change to women's clothes—had been made on Palm Sunday, March 25. The ordinary trial opened on Tuesday in Holy Week, March 27. The seventy articles of accusation were read to the prisoner on Tuesday and Wednesday in Holy Week, March 27 and 28. Then Jeanne was left in her cell until Holy Saturday. This gave her plenty of time to experience in her soul the mysteries of Maundy Thursday and Good Friday, March 29 and 30. The sufferings and death of her Lord could not be without meaning for her own pain and anguish. On Holy Saturday, March 31, she was confronted with more questions about the Church militant. But she well knew that Easter Sunday commemorates the triumph of Christ over sin and death. Even deprived of the Easter Sunday liturgy on April 1, she could well live the mystery of the resurrection in her heart, with or without the felt presence of angels and saints.

From then on, however, Jeanne was inexorably led on the way to her martyrdom.

Charitable Exhortations

The Easter season was marked for Jeanne by the charitable exhortations to which she was subjected. The first was made on April 18, the second on May 2. On May 9 Jeanne was taken to the torture chamber in the hope that she would break down and admit her guilt. A last charitable exhortation took place on May 23, when the twelve articles of which she was finally found guilty were read to her. The charges against her that touch on angels and saints were listed in our previous chapter. The remaining charges were as follows:

Article five, on wearing male dress: "The clerics say that in this you blaspheme God and despise him in his sacraments; you disobey divine law, Sacred Scripture, and canonical decisions; you think wrongly and err in faith; you boast vainly, and you are suspect of idolatry and hatred of self and of your [female] garments, in imitation of pagan customs."[78]

Article six, on her standard: ". . . you cruelly want the shedding of human blood . . . blaspheming God in his commandments and revelations."

Article seven, on what led her to Robert de Baudricourt: ". . . you were impious toward your parents, disobeying God's command to honor one's parents, scandalous, blaspheming God, erring in faith, and you made a presumptuous and temerarious promise" [to keep her virginity].

Article eight, on leaping from the tower of Beaurevoir: ". . . in this there was pusillanimity verging on despair and equivalently on suicide . . . and you think wrongly of human free will *(de libertate humani arbitrii)."*

Article ten, concerning the claim that Jeanne knows by revelation that God loves certain persons more than herself, and that her two saints speak French and not English because they are not of the English party, and that once she knew that her voices were for her king she did not love the Burgundians: "The clerics say that this is a temerarious, excessive, and presumptuous assertion, a superstitious divination, a blasphemy against St. Catherine and St. Marguerite, a transgression of the precept of the love of neighbor."

Article twelve, concerning her statements in general and her view of the Church militant: "The clerics say that you are schismatic, you think wrongly of the unity and authority of the Church, you are apostate, and so far you pertinaciously err in faith."

These articles did not function as points for the prosecution that could be rebutted by the defense, if there had been one. They already were the tribunal's conclusions. Prosecutors and judges were indistinguishable. Since the tribunal had found Jeanne *la Pucelle* guilty on these twelve counts there was now no escape. The machinery set up by the bishop of Beauvais to destroy her was working as planned, if less brilliantly than he had expected. Jeanne would never again urge Charles VII and inspire French soldiers to fight the armies of the duke of Bedford. It

[78]All the articles are in T, 1:375–80.

only remained to determine if she would spend the rest of her life in prison fed on bread and water or if she would die at the stake. She would suffer a slow death by progressive starvation or a swift death by fire and smoke. On May 23, therefore, after the twelve points had been read to her Jeanne was admonished that she must retract what she had said on all of them or face the consequence, death by fire. The mellifluous speech of Canon Pierre Maurice began with the words, *Johanna, amica carissima . . .* "Jeanne, dearest friend. . . ."[79]

A Deadly Choice

Jeanne was thus faced with the deadly choice of retraction or obstinacy. Retractation would have implied the denial that she had ever seen angels and saints, that the Lord Christ had sent these angels and saints to her, that she had been given a divine mission. It would have meant pleading guilty of witchcraft and heresy and throwing herself on the mercy of the court to spare her life because she repented. Such a plea would have led inexorably to doing penance for the rest of her life in a church prison. Obstinacy would have signified that she persevered in what the tribunal had identified as witchcraft, blasphemy, and heresy. It would entail the same punishment of life imprisonment. Neither, of course, would have satisfied the duke of Bedford or the bishop of Beauvais. They wanted her dead. And to this end they—or rather the bishop—had to push her to pay lip service to repentance and then to retract it. Since this was the intended purpose of the reduced list of twelve articles, these were centered on what the accusation perceived to be the weakest links in her case.

An unmistakable aspect of Jeanne's holiness shines precisely in her serenity in the face of the unexpected. It is unusual to have visions of angels and saints and to hear their voices. Jeanne of course realized it, and this is why she was frightened the first time it happened. It is still more unusual for a young girl

---

[79]The admonestation was of course made in French; it is given in Latin in the acts: T, 1:380–83.

to be sent, be it by celestial messengers, on a political and military mission of national and international dimensions that involved the reunification of one country and the relations between two powerful kingdoms. Jeanne had found herself suddenly changed in her heart at the moment when she promised to keep her virginity for as long as it would please God. Likewise, once she had received her temporal mission this mission was never abolished or modified, even when Jeanne was not sure what her next course of action ought to be.

Yet the angels and saints whose voices she heard never forced her to do anything. As was the case with the Virgin Mary at the annunciation, Jeanne's agreement was necessary. Without her consent nothing unusual would have happened. Jeanne Romée would have led the ordinary life of a peasant woman in a small frontier village. How the kingdom of France would have fared is uncertain. How long the great war between the French and English monarchies would have lasted and how it would have ended is of course entirely unknown.

SEVEN

The Darkening Night

The way of Jeanne *la Pucelle* has been so far a way of spiritual light. There is light with the voices that speak to her in her heart as she joyfully listens to what God tells her through the angelic messengers and the saints in heaven, in her behavior as she relates with simplicity and frankness to all who meet her—king, men-at-arms, ladies of high society, ordinary women of the people, babies for whom she acts as godmother. There is light in the chapels and churches she enters to attend Mass and to pray. There is light in her prayer when she speaks to God: "Most sweet God, in honor of your holy Passion, I ask you, if you love me . . ." All these lights are experienced as joy, a joy that still pierces through the formalities of questions and responses at her trial.

The light that Jeanne experienced was for the eyes of her soul. Yet it also transformed her perception of the world. Bells ringing meant the proclamation of the divine presence, and often she heard her voices at that very moment. Meeting with the dauphin meant seeing the one who was destined to be sacramentally anointed as the representative of the king of heaven for the kingdom of France. Spending time with the companions of her journeys and with the good people, men and women, who supported her meant communing in the holy purpose of serving the designs of God. It also transformed her perception of the Church, for though she knew that the English leaders wanted to kill her, she never really believed, until it was too late to change the course of events, that a bishop and some university scholars shared the same purpose.

Rippling Shadows

Ripples of shadows indeed spread from time to time through her soul, as when Jeanne experienced the side effects of war in her village and when she was shaken by the first visit of the archangel and surprised by the unusual mission she received from heaven, when she left her parents in Domremy with only a partial explanation of where she was going, when she found skepticism in Baudricourt and secret opposition in the king's entourage, when she had to argue with military leaders about the nature of the war and the urgency of offensive and when she perceived that the king preferred talk and diplomacy to pushing out the enemy at the tip of the lance, when she saw wounded men, French or English, lying on the battlefield, when she heard men swearing and saw loose women waiting for soldiers, when priests—the pastor of Vaucouleurs, Brother Richard under the walls of Troyes—threw holy water at her, when canon lawyers and theologians—first at Poitiers, later in Rouen—tried to probe into her soul, when matrons were delegated by the authorities to probe into her body for proof of virginity. All such shadows were still small enough not to last very long and to vanish as soon as Jeanne cleansed her soul in confession, which she did on all possible occasions. They were little compared to the great onslaughts of her martyrdom: "I call martyrdom," Jeanne patiently explained, "the pain and adversity that I suffer in my prison."[1]

Darker shadows must have formed in the uncertainty that followed the king's coronation. Although it was done without much preparation and in a hurry, the crowning on July 17, 1429, was of course the high point of Jeanne's public life, the deliverance of Orléans having preluded it as the sign that the dauphin should dare to cross through Burgundian territory to go to Reims. From this high point Jeanne's way could only lead downward unless she received instructions from God's counsel as to what was to follow the king's triumph in Reims. From a military point of view, the reconquest of the kingdom was under way, and it had to be actively pursued if the recent gains were not to be lost. But the archangel and the saints who had brought *la Pucelle*

[1]T, 1:148.

thus far did not indicate what her role should be in the months or years to come. From what Jeanne expressly said to the archbishop of Reims and to Dunois when the royal army arrived at La Ferté and Crépy-en-Valois, her task was done: "May it please God my Creator to let me go now, abandon weaponry, and go back to my father and my mother, watching their sheep with my sister and my brothers, who would be happy to see me."[2]

Charles VII, however, was not ready to let her go. She was an asset he wished to keep by his side even while he was negotiating, against her advice, with his adversary Philippe *le Bon*. For a few weeks one could have the impression that Charles was about to conquer the Burgundian cities that lay to the east and the north of Paris. He entered Compiègne accompanied by Jeanne on August 18. But already his agents were leading secret negotiations with representatives of the duke of Burgundy, and a short truce was agreed upon on August 28. On expiration of the truce Jeanne and the duke of Alençon moved to St.-Denys by way of Senlis, and then marched south toward Paris to probe the defenses of the city. Their assault on porte St.-Honoré and porte St.-Denys failed on September 8. This done, Charles VII wanted no more fighting. More truces were signed covering longer periods, and though they were limited to certain areas, these included Paris. Having withdrawn to St.-Denys, Jeanne deposited an armor and a sword in the great church[3] (September 11 or 12). This was to honor St. Denys, in keeping with a military custom.

Meanwhile the king returned to the Loire valley. At Gien on September 21 he disbanded the bulk of the army, thus indicating that, until further notice, diplomacy would prevail over war. Precisely, this became Jeanne's dilemma: Her voices had not prepared her for a life of leisure at the court. In the following period Jeanne continued to hear the voices of her two saints, but they gave no direction concerning her mission. Jeanne moved around with the king through October. But she did not relish life at the court. She kept her small military house, with d'Aulun, her two pages, her two brothers, and probably a few others. The king still paid for it.

[2]Q, 3:14–15.
[3]T, 1:78.

In November 1429 Jeanne was sent by the king, along with Jean d'Alençon, to St.-Pierre-le-Moûtier. She had a major role in the storming of the walls. After a few days of rest in Moulins she joined several captains before the walls of La Charité-sur-Loire. This city used to be a Burgundian stronghold, but it was now held by a warlord, Périnet Gressart, who recognized no sovereign. After a month-long siege the French troops tried and failed on November 24 to scale the walls of the town. They pulled back, quite possibly because the captains judged their numbers and equipment insufficient for the undertaking. It was in that period, on December 29, that king Charles signed the decree that ennobled Jeanne's family and their descendants. But this was little consolation for her. What was now missing was the kind of master plan that had led *la Pucelle* to Chinon, Orléans, and Reims. Jeanne was weaned of the lights she had grown accustomed to.

In April 1430 Jeanne left the court at Sully-sur-Loire to go north and join the captains who were harassing the English and Burgundians near Paris. It must have been around that time that Jeanne obtained a fighting force of a few hundred men that she could lead to areas not included in the current truce. The bulk of this troop was made of Italian mercenaries commanded by a minor condottiere, Bartolomeo Baretta.[4] After leaving Sully-sur-Loire Jeanne's column marched toward Lagny, a short distance east of Paris, where it fought in April. That is where Jeanne prayed with the girls of the town that a three-day-old baby come back to life.[5] That is also where a certain Franquet d'Arras was captured,[6] whom Jeanne wanted to exchange for an Armagnac prisoner of the English. From Lagny the corps went south to Melun.

----

[4]Champion, *Guillaume,* 38, note 2. The same page gives the names of some of Jeanne's other companions: Jean Foucaut, Alain Giron, Ambroise de Loré, Geoffroy de Saint-Belin, Poton de Xaintrailles, Rigaud de Fontaines, Jacques de Chabagne, Poton le Bourguignon, and a Scotsman, Hughe de Kennedy.

[5]3/3, T, 1:103.

[6]3/14: T, 1:151.

Foreknowledge of Capture

It was at Melun on Easter Sunday of 1430 that Jeanne learned from her voices that she would be captured by the enemy "before the feast of St. John."[7] Easter Sunday was on April 23, and the feast in question must be the Nativity of John the Baptist, on June 24. Now there were three ways in which Jeanne could be caught: in the course of a regular battle; in an unexpected ambush during a march; or anywhere by treason. As she confided to Girardin d'Epinal when they met at Châlons on the way to Reims, she was afraid only of treason.[8] Such a fear was realistic. Jeanne kept her eyes open and she knew that the service of the king was often halfhearted. Should advantages be found on the side of Henry VI, there were many who would switch allegiance. It was part of the general confusion of her times that just as one could choose which pope to recognize, it was also possible to choose one's king. That this would be treason on the part of those who had given their fealty to the legitimate line of kingship did not weigh heavily on many consciences. And since Jeanne was aware of this as well as anybody, she could only suffer from it in her mind and soul even if she was not directly the victim of treason. She did run into treason under the walls of Soissons when Guichard Bournel, the governor, who was sold to the duke of Burgundy, refused to open the city gates,[9] although this was directed at Charles VII rather than at her.

To avoid being caught, increased and constant protection by the men of her household was always possible. To escape an ambush it was safer to travel in a large group than a small one and to send scouts in several directions. The size of the contingents that were with Jeanne has been estimated at several hundred to four thousand. In most circumstances this would be sufficient to avoid an ambush. As to being made prisoner in the course of a battle, extreme caution not to be separated from the soldiers was imperious. Extreme caution, however, was not among Jeanne's strong points. And even though she never used her sword, her tactic in battle was more offensive than defensive.

[7]3/10: T, 1:111–12.
[8]Q, 2:423.
[9]There is an allusion to this on 3/3: T, 1:108.

She drove toward the enemy, hoping to draw the soldiers with her. And as she made herself extremely visible, nothing could dissipate the danger of a pinpointed maneuver against herself. This was an inescapable dimension of the growing night that was now engulfing *la Pucelle*.

The Expectation of Captivity

It is altogether remarkable that during what could have been a period of debilitating fear and anxious apprehension Jeanne did not shun the possible occasions to be caught. Her attitude to the prospect of captivity was two sided.

On the one hand, of course, she did not like the idea. As she readily admitted on March 3, "I would prefer to give my soul back to God than to be in the hands of the English."[10] Again on March 14 she explained why she tried to escape from Beaurevoir: "She knew that she was sold to the English and she would have preferred to die rather than be in the hands of the English, her adversaries."[11] She loathed it when the voices hinted that she would see the king of England: "You will not be freed before seeing the king of the English."[12] To which Jeanne objected, "Truly I would not want to see him, and I would prefer to die than to be in the hands of the English." It was precisely when she learned that English emissaries were on the way to the castle of Beaurevoir to discuss terms with Jean de Luxembourg that she decided, against her voices' advice, to take the jump from a tower window and attempt to run away.

On the other hand, however, Jeanne simply, as she always did, accepted the designs of God and the doings of divine Providence. Since her calling was from God, the mission she had re-

[10]T, 1:107.

[11]3/14: T, 1:144.

[12]3/28: T, 1:243. Jeanne never saw Henry VI, but it is quite possible that the young king saw her. He was brought to Rouen by his uncle the duke of Bedford about the same time as Jeanne. It would be surprising if the duke had not wanted the king to catch a glimpse of his most dangerous enemy subdued. It would have been beneath the king's dignity to appear at the trial, but it would have been easy for him to observe Jeanne being led in and out of prison.

ceived was "a kind of ministry"[13] She was ready to welcome all its conditions. Even her English captivity could be seen in the perspective of divine Providence. She therefore took to heart the voices' advice:

> It was said to her that she would be taken before the feast of St. John, that this had to be, that she should not be surprised but take everything in good part, and that God would help her.[14]

This was sufficient to ensure that *la Pucelle* keep her peace of soul amid the uncertainty of not knowing the where, when, and to what end of her capture. She told no one about it. Nobody in the nullity inquiry betrayed any awareness of Jeanne's foreknowledge of her coming captivity. As the revelation of her mission and its success had been treasured in her heart and mind, so was the anticipation of defeat. It became part of her secret, locked in that room of her soul that was shared only with angels and saints of heaven. Her voices kept the thought of capture alive in her mind as they repeated their warning "several times and nearly every day." Jeanne made no protest except to say that she did not wish to see the king of England. Yet even then she did not complain about the will of God. Glory and humiliation were both given by the Lord and were therefore, whatever misgivings Jeanne may have had, equally to be cherished.

Admittedly the princes that she got to know did not regard captivity as the ultimate catastrophe, since a ransom was usually set by the captors and was eventually paid. Jean d'Alençon, captured in 1424 at the battle of Verneuil, had been released in 1427 on his promise to pay a ransom of 200,000 gold *saluts,* but, the ransom paid, he was on the brink of ruin. La Hire himself had been a prisoner in English hands shortly after the battle of Verneuil, but he was released in 1427. In any case, the English leaders could be slow to agree to a ransom. For Charles d'Orléans, fifteen years after his capture at Azincourt no ransom had yet been set. Despite her old-fashioned conception of chivalry, Jeanne was a realist. If she was treated normally like a person of importance Charles VII would be informed of what he had to pay to get her back. She

---

13. . . . *de facto suo erat quoddam ministerium:* Q, 2:110.
14T, 1:144.

could be confident that he would accept whatever terms were set. But she knew well enough that in spite of the recent ennoblement of her kin she was really a commoner, and there was no guarantee that she would be held for ransom. Ordinary prisoners for whom no ransom could be expected were often massacred. Or she could be held in prison indefinitely. This was why she requested of her saints "that when she was taken she would die soon without long travail in prison." But the voices repeated what from the beginning had been the central line of their spiritual guidance of *la Pucelle:* "that she take everything in good part, and that so it had to be."

Pangs of Ambiguity

Jeanne waited one month for the fulfillment of her voices' prophecy, for she was captured on May 23, 1429, toward six in the afternoon. During this long expectation she had to live on two levels. On the outside she functioned normally in the world of everyday occurrences. In conjunction with the captains, who kept abreast of the overall military situation as well as of the king's diplomatic projects, she sought to orient the expedition toward the cities that were the most threatened by the enemy. Meanwhile, within herself she pondered the knowledge that her days of active service were coming to an end. The machinery of her mission was grinding down, though not in idle leisure. The best way to fill the time that separated her from captivity was to pursue the good purpose for which she had been called out of her village: aiding to the recovery of the kingdom while she waited for what had to be.

To an alien observer the itinerary of the expeditionary corps may well seem haphazard, like that of an underground unit (as in the French *maquis* of World War II) looking for suitable coups against the army of occupation. From Melun the troop traveled north to Lagny-sur-Marne,[15] between Paris and Meaux, then further north to Senlis, Borenglise (Elincourt), Compiègne, south to Pont-Ste-Maxence,[16] back to Compiègne, to Soissons

[15]I give the itinerary as outlined in Q, 5:377–82. A slightly different sequence is given in Sackville-West, *Saint Joan of Arc,* 377–80.

[16]Called Pont-l'Evêque in the trial; it is a bridge town and fortress on the Oise river, north of Senlis. The expedition, around May 15, was aimed

The Darkening Night 139

where Guichard Bournel refused to open the gates and no attempt was made to storm the walls, to Compiègne, then southwest to Lagny again, Crépy-en-Valois (May 22), and back north
during the night to Compiègne. From the end of April to the
day Jeanne was captured Compiègne was the center of opera-
tions, from which the soldiers sallied forth for raids on the enemy
and to which they returned.

Jeanne must have learned many things during this period,
and not only the art of patiently waiting for the unfolding of her
destiny. Sensitive as she was to the necessity of cleansing one's
conscience, she could not be blind to the moral shortcomings of
her entourage. The very nature of war as it was led in this post-
coronation phase when the king was more intent on diplomacy
than on fighting must have made her realize how frail was the
human basis on which to construct the kingdom of France as
Christ's kingdom through his anointed delegate. At Lagny when
Jeanne was informed that the man—an innkeeper from Paris—
for whom she planned to exchange Franquet d'Arras had died,
she abandoned her prisoner to human justice because he was
known to be a bandit and a murderer.[17] But she could also discover, undoubtedly to her dismay, that most of her own allies
were of the same metal as Franquet. The ideal of knighthood was
no longer actively pursued.

Jeanne of course could not know that Gilles de Rais would
become a sadistic criminal who would relish killing children, that
her "genteel duke," Jean d'Alençon, would later negotiate with
the duke of Bedford and, twice condemned to death for high
treason, be twice pardoned by Charles VII. Nor could she guess
that Guillaume de Flavy (ca. 1398–1449), the commander of
Compiègne and a solid adversary of the Burgundians, would ter-
rorize the countryside and neighboring cities, notably Noyon
and Soissons.[18] The future of her companions was not revealed

---

at the Burgundians, who were laying siege to the nearby town and fortress
of Choisy. It failed to dislodge them: Champion, *Guillaume*, 39–41.

[17]3/14: T, 1:151.

[18]In July 1436 Guillaume de Flavy (ca.1398–1449) married a ten-year-
old child, Blanche d'Overbreuc (1426–after 1500); in spite of his promise
not to consummate the marriage for three years, he did so after a few weeks;
for years he beat and terrorized his wife, openly flaunting his dalliance with

to Jeanne and she was herself too clean-minded to suspect it. Yet she was by no means naive, and she must have realized that those who served the cause of Charles VII with her were never committed to her ideal of a holy monarchy, or if they somehow saw this as an ideal it had little impact on their behavior as soon as they were away from her. They were in the business of war. For some, like Baretta and his mercenaries, this was a way of life that afforded excitement and opportunities for looting and wenching. For those of high nobility like the duke of Alençon as Jeanne knew him, fighting was an extension of life at court, in the same category as hunting, and it was haloed by the honor that could be gained in the king's service. For those in between like Poton de Xaintrailles or Jean de Vignolles, a soldier's life was an unstable mixture of cruelty, exploitation, courage, fealty, and indifference to danger.

Jeanne, however, was not in the habit of attributing evil purposes to others. When she was asked if "those of your party firmly believe that you have been sent by God," she answered: "I do not know if they believe it and I refer to their conscience; but if they do not believe it I still have been sent by God."[19] Jeanne did react with indignation at the public contempt of God when men took God's name in vain and when whores were welcome attendants of the army. If she noticed evil or suspected some hidden form of it she invited the soldiers to penance and the sacrament of reconciliation, and she urged them to attend the daily prayer service organized for them by the clergy. But she could not ignore that with or without the sacrament the perpetrators of grave crimes, including murder and all sorts of spoliations, could beg the king for an "act of abolition." Parliaments and courts were not usually lenient toward criminals, even high-placed ones, but Charles VII was remarkably tolerant and forgiving, and he seldom forgot past services. His reconquest of the

---

several mistresses. He was assassinated on March 9, 1449, by two of his servants at the request of Blanche, who was pardoned by the king in 1450. Blanche then married her lover Pierre de Louvain, who was himself murdered in 1564 by Raoul de Flavy, Guillaume's brother: Champion, *Guillaume,* 77–111.

[19] 3/3: T, 1:99.

Burgundian and English areas was systematically accompanied by letters of pardon for those who had opposed his reign. No measures were ever taken against those who had enriched themselves in the service of Henry VI. In this basically forgiving attitude King Charles VII was not unlike Jeanne.[20] She respected consciences; she did not presume to speak for others; she tried to lead them to God, but then she let them face God as they could. Yet the ambiguity of military life must have laid a heavy burden on the virginity of her soul.

Rendezvous with Capture

La Pucelle made no attempt to take protective measures that might possibly delay her capture. Since becoming a prisoner was the will of the Lord, it was an event that should be, if not hastened, at least facilitated. Already at Orléans Jeanne made herself highly visible as she went into combat. She sought neither to hide behind a range of heavily armed soldiers nor to stay in the arrear. On the contrary, she went forward with her standard so that the soldiers could see where she was. Whether she held her standard or it was carried by a soldier, it acted as a rallying point for the French and by the same token as a telltale sign of her exact location for the Burgundians and English. It was also presumably for the purpose of high visibility that Jeanne acquired the habit of dressing up for battle in strikingly colorful garments, in the fashion of the high nobility. Wealthy and titled aristocrats wished to be recognized by the enemy, so that if they lost the fight they might be taken alive for ransom rather than slaughtered. Jeanne learned to dress like them, her white steel armor covered with a *huque* of colored cloth, usually dark green, the color of Orléans, long sleeves dangling by her sides. One cannot exclude that in some way she wished to help her captor recognize her and so fulfill his destiny and her own.

[20]The king of England, Henry V, had insisted, like Jeanne, on an army discipline that strictly forbade swearing and looting. Like her he was convinced that his cause was divine. Unlike her he was led by personal ambition, and at Azincourt he ordered the slaughter of prisoners. For this reason some historians have called him Henry the Cutthroat.

The morning of May 23 had been spent resting, for Jeanne, Baretta, and a group of his mercenaries, along with Jeanne's usual guard, had ridden from Crépy-en-Valois during the night.[21] Toward the end of the afternoon the governor of Compiègne, Guillaume de Flavy, and Jeanne led a small group to an isolated Burgundian outpost commanded by Baudot de Noyelles. This was not a rash undertaking, and the post was destroyed. But the action had been observed by Jean de Luxembourg from the top of a hill. As the unit returned to Compiègne it was attacked by Burgundians who rushed in from the village of Clairois. In the course of the ensuing combat Jeanne with a few of her men ploughed deep into Burgundian ranks. Three times they were able to attack in this manner and then to disengage. Then, either the noise of battle or a call for help from Jean de Luxembourg brought in an English contingent from the village of Venette; following the bank of the Oise river they cut off the retreat to Compiègne.

Some of Jeanne's soldiers panicked when they realized what was happening; others were able to fight their way through over the drawbridge, Flavy among them; others still took to boats and crossed the river. But as some of the pursuing English were also about to storm the drawbridge, it was lifted up and nobody else could pass. Jeanne was left behind with a small fighting group. Several foot soldiers from the Burgundians attacked her at the same time, and she was pulled down from her horse by an archer. This man was from the "lance" of the bâtard de Wandomme, who served under Jean de Luxembourg.[22] Jean

---

[21]Using details given by the Burgundian chronicler Monstrelet, Champion describes the group as comprising "thirty-two men-at-arms, forty-three crossbowmen, twenty archers," plus Jeanne's brother Pierre du Lys, her chaplain Pasquerel, Poton the Burgundian, and two pages: Champion, *Guillaume,* 44. Louis de Coutes must have been one of the pages; the unknown other must have been a replacement for Raymond, who had been killed during the assault on Paris.

[22]I sum up here the account given in Champion, *Guillaume,* who draws on Burgundian chronicles (45–47). According to Monstrelet the Burgundian-English side would have counted five thousand soldiers. Perceval de Cagny reports that some of her men called on Jeanne to pull back: *Mettez peine de recouvrer la ville ou nous somme perdus!* ("Hurry back

d'Aulon, her brother Pierre du Lys, and her chaplain Pasquerel were also taken. It was about six in the evening, nearly night.[23]

Jeanne's First Captivity

Hitherto Jeanne's Christian life had been quite simple. Since the age of thirteen virginity of body and soul came to her effortlessly. "She was chaste," simply said Jean d'Alençon.[24] Courage and endurance were inseparable from her daily life when she was with the army in campaign. Friendliness and charity marked her behavior in her occasional sojourns at court or in the palaces of the nobility or the high bourgeoisie where distinguished ladies received her. Her piety was deep and fervent without being ostentatious or obnoxious: "Several times," Jean d'Alençon testified, "I saw her receive the body of Christ; when she saw the host she shed many tears. She received the holy Eucharist twice a week and she went to confession

---

to the city or we are lost!"), and she gave an answer that is typical of her general view of fighting: *Taisez-vous! Il ne tendra qu'à vous qu'ils ne soient déconfis. Ne pensez que de férir sur eux* ("Shut up! It only depends on you that they be beaten. Think only of striking at them") (46, n. 7).

[23]Already in the fifteenth century Guillaume de Flavy was accused of high treason by François de Rieux, whose father, Pierre de Rieux, *maréchal* of France, he had kidnapped, sequestrated, and left to die. The accusation was picked up in vaguer terms by several chronicles. Admittedly, Guillaume had family ties with the Burgundian party. His two older brothers fought Charles VII, but he and his younger brothers fought Henry VI. At any rate, I do not think Guillaume de Flavy was guilty of treason if he was the one who ordered the drawbridge of Compiègne lifted. Jeanne does not seem to have been in a position to arrive at the drawbridge before the English contingent. Given her offensive style of fighting she may not even have tried. Her efforts to maintain the offensive effectively covered the retreat of those who made it back within the walls. Quite other was the case of Soissons when Guichard Bournel refused to open the gates. Guichard had an agreement with Philippe *le Bon,* for which he was duly paid. The Benedictine Placide Bertheau in 1654 gave what seems to me the correct version: "One cannot legitimately attribute the cause of her disaster to anything else than an excessive desire to save the others, that resulted in her own loss." All this is discussed in Champion, *Guillaume,* appendix 1, pp. 281–86.

[24]Q, 3:98.

often."[25] Clearly, Jeanne shared the assumption of popular medieval piety that the Eucharist is not only to be received as the Body of Christ but is also to be contemplated by looking at the consecrated host, as when it is raised at the elevation and shown at Communion time, and also when it is occasionally exposed for worship or carried in procession on the feast of Corpus Christi. And so when Jeanne saw the host she wept. According to the circumstance and grace of the moment these tears could be tears of love, of joy, of thanksgiving, of penance. Even in the dangerous days of the journey to Chinon when her escort led Jeanne carefully through enemy territory, she would have liked to stop for Mass: "If we could hear the Mass we would do well."[26] Jean de Nouillonpont adds that they stopped only twice for Mass because of the danger. Once it was in the cathedral of Auxerre.

Jeanne was simple, straightforward, and humble. Everyone who spoke about her in the nullity investigation so testified. Jean de Nouillonpont himself added: "Yes, *la Pucelle* went most willingly to Mass; she went to confession frequently, she gave alms; very often she entrusted money to me to give it in the name of God. As long as I was in her company I knew her to be good, simple, pious, a good Christian, well-thinking *(bien tournée)* and God-fearing." One of the most absurd articles of accusation in the list of seventy—article 53—is the one that found her seething with unlawful pride:

> Against the precepts of God and the saints the said Jeanne with presumption and pride assumed domination in and over men, constituting herself the head and leader of an army that sometimes had sixteen thousand men, in which there were princes, barons and many other noblemen, all of whom she made to serve under her as their principal captain.[27]

There is in this a factual error, since Jeanne was never the commander-in-chief of any army. In addition, she denied writing

[25]Q, 3:99.
[26]Q, 3:100.
[27]3/28: T, 1:262. This contention was not kept in the final list of twelve articles of accusation.

to the duke of Bedford that she was *chef de guerre,* though when the article was read to her she added, "and if I were *chef de guerre,* it would have been to beat the English."[28] The idea is implicit that this would have been a good enough reason. But whatever her actual function with the soldiers and their leaders, Jeanne never dominated anyone. She never took pride in herself, in the mission she had received, in the revelations that were made to her. A lesser soul could have felt a tinge of pride. She did not. Here again, the main line of her spirituality was self-abandonment. She was simply God's handmaid, "*la Pucelle,* daughter of God."

At the same time, however, Jeanne could not but suffer from sensing shadows of mediocrity and streaks of occasional evil in the all-too-human elements that hemmed her in. From the moment she was captured these shadows could only darken and lengthen. The friendship of the ladies in Jean de Luxembourg's household could not compensate Jeanne's realization that she herself had become a political asset for which the comte de Ligny, Philippe de Bourgogne, and John of Lancaster were bargaining. She could not know that the University of Paris and the bishop of Beauvais were also jousting for the prize they wanted— her body to burn—in a game that was no less political and deadly for having an ecclesiastical coloring. For a few months, as long as she was in the hands of Jean de Luxembourg, Jeanne was treated like a distinguished prisoner of war. But from the moment at Beaurevoir when she learned that English emissaries were coming to discuss the terms offered by the duke of Bedford to buy her she could hardly expect anything better than a harsh prison.

It was Jeanne's last heroic action in the armies of Charles VII that led her to captivity. With the end of her military actions the role of her voices changed. Jeanne, however, reported very little about what they said during the first months of her captivity in the manors of Jean de Luxembourg. The most we know relates to their urgings when Jeanne thought of leaping to freedom. They told her not to jump. They tried to teach her patience.

[28]. . . . *et si j'étais chef de guerre, c'était pour battre les anglais.* In this sentence the imperfect has a conditional sense: "Had I been . . . it would have been. . . ."

Jeanne's interrogators in Rouen exploited against her the fact that she jumped from the tower of Beaurevoir. They interpreted this as an attempted suicide, which they attributed to the sin of despair. This became article 41 in the list of seventy, and 8 in the list of twelve submitted to the assessors and to the University of Paris. The first version is very involved:

> . . . the said Jeanne being desperate, in hatred and contempt of the English and also because of the destruction of Compiègne that she had heard was going to happen, attempted to jump from the top of a high tower, and at the devil's suggestion she put this project into her mind, she applied herself to doing it, and she did what in fact she could by jumping, being so impelled and led by a diabolical instinct, which she intended for the liberation of the bodies rather than the souls of herself and many others, she boasting many times that she would kill herself rather than allow herself to be traded into the hands of the English.[29]

The second version is more straightforward and factual:

> The said woman says and confesses that, not being forced or pushed by anyone, she jumped from a very high tower, preferring to die rather than be traded into the hands of her adversaries and rather than live after the destruction of Compiègne. She also says that she could not avoid this fall, and yet the said saints Catherine and Marguerite had forbidden her to jump. She says that this offense against them is a great sin, but she knows well that this sin was forgiven after she confessed it. And she says that she knows this by revelation.[30]

The point is summed up as follows in the final forms of the twelve articles. Article 8: ". . . the clerics say that in this there was pusillanimity leading to despair, which means *[interpretative]* to killing yourself; and also in this you made a temerarious and presumptuous assertion as regards the forgiveness that you claim to have of this sin; and you are in error concerning the freedom of human choice."[31] This last consideration is broad-

---

[29]3/28: T, 1:242.
[30]T, 1:294.
[31]5/23: T, 1:378: . . . *male sentis de libertate humani arbitrii* (literally, "you think wrongly on the freedom of human choice").

ened in article 9: ". . . you are in error concerning the Christian faith."[32]

The broad accusation of heresy tallies with the bishop's contention that Jeanne's defense of her male clothes amounts to disobedience to the Church's ordinary teaching. But the accusation of heresy "concerning freedom of human choice" makes little sense. One may assume that "human choice" has the same sense as *liberum arbitrium,* the human capacity to choose among diverse courses of action. In the theology derived from St. Augustine, which generally prevailed in the schools, this capacity is fully adequate for choices that have no moral relevance, but it is insufficient to make a morally good option, since the human will is inclined to evil by virtue of original sin. The assistance of divine grace is necessary both for the initiative of conversion and all along the converted life. This was of course discussed in the schools of theology, and there were differences between the more classical theologians and those who belonged to the recent school of the Franciscan William of Ockham (ca. 1300–ca. 1350) and the nominalists. In the latter perspective the incapacity of the human will to deserve grace and do good works is not absolute. It is relative to the will of God, who has so decreed for the present world. Yet God could have organized creation differently. In the jargon of the schools the necessity of divine grace is correct *de potentia ordinata,* not *de potentia absoluta.* Jeanne, however, knew nothing of such distinctions. She had heard Franciscan friars preach, and some of them may have underlined the freedom of the will in a somewhat nominalist direction. But there is nothing in Jeanne's responses that can suggest an erroneous notion of grace and free will. On the contrary, she manifestly showed that in all things she wanted to rely on the grace of God.

What seems to stand behind this peculiar charge is the alleged statement included in the formal presentation of article 8 on April 5: "She also says that she could not avoid this fall [from the tower]."[33] This had provoked no questions in Rouen. It was in the comments of the faculty of theology of the University of

---

[32]. . . *male sentis in fide christiana.* T, 1:379.

[33]T, 1:294. There is no mention here of wrong thinking in the matter of freedom of choice.

Paris that the charge of error concerning freedom of the will was formulated for the first time;[34] the comments of the faculty of canon law contained no similar accusation. In any case, Bishop Cauchon must have welcomed this new charge even if it was unsubstantiated, since he kept it in the final version of the articles of accusation. Thus he betrayed a basic flaw in his method: even though no intrinsic argument, in the eyes of the judges, established that Jeanne erred in faith in regard to human freedom, it became one of the points on which her condemnation as a heretic was based, and this on the purely extrinsic evidence that it was listed by the University of Paris.

Was Jeanne led by despair to an attempted suicide? She firmly denied it. Certainly she did not want to be sold to the English any more than she wished to see the king of England. She felt so strongly about it that she did not follow her voices' advice. But she was also aware, as she stated, of a rumor that Compiègne, though vigorously defended by Guillaume de Flavy, would soon fall to the English-Burgundian coalition and that the conquest of the city would be followed by a general slaughter. The precedent for this was the fall of Paris on May 29, 1418, and the ensuing massacre of the Armagnacs. Jeanne could not ignore this. And if she could prevent the massacre she thought she should do it. Justice was in her eyes the central political virtue. To protect the feeble and endangered was part of the oath of knighthood. Therefore it was her duty to try to escape, as long as her voices did not outright forbid it. They did not, though their clear advice was not to jump. If Jeanne disregarded their recommendation it was in view of the primacy of justice. Two other principles she held dear could be seen to support her decision. The first was "Our Lord the first served."[35] Surely in her mind it would be a better service of the Lord to rush to the help of the people of Compiègne than to remain in idleness with the remaining lady of Beaurevoir, Jeanne de Béthune, whose husband was planning to sell her to the king of England. The second principle was the French proverb "Help yourself; the Lord will help you," from which her conception of war derived:

---

[34]T, 1:362
[35]3/31: Holy Saturday: T, 1:288.

"In God's name, the soldiers will fight and God will give the victory."[36]

In the turmoil that certainly went on in her soul as she debated these matters, Jeanne never gave up her full confidence in the Lord's guidance and her total love for God. When she realized that the death of Jeanne de Luxembourg had removed the main obstacle to her being sold to the duke of Bedford, she kept her full trust in the Lord even though she was terribly upset. She constantly denied that her Lord, the king of heaven, had ever let her down. But the struggle between her unflinching total trust in God and her fully human mistrust of the English and their king could not but tear her apart. Love of God and attention to her voices had to take the heroic colors of trust in spite of evidence. At the worst moments of the itinerary along which she was led under guard from Beauregard to Rouen and of her ensuing captivity she continued to practice trust and love of God to a heroic degree. Abandoned to all appearances by everyone, she remained faithful to her self-abandonment in God's hands.

Jeanne's Second Captivity

Of Jeanne's itinerary to Rouen we have no other details than names of towns and fortresses. In November 1530 she went through Arras, St.-Riquier, Drugy, Le Crotoy; in December through St.-Valéry, Eu, Dieppe, arriving in Rouen around Christmas.[37] There was no time lost. The trial started on January 9, 1431. The first interrogation of Jeanne took place on February 21.

The conditions of her captivity in the castle of Rouen were harsh. She was held in an English prison with two or three English guards commanded by a certain John Grey, who were always inside her cell. Her legs were chained to a heavy log. Jeanne's state of mind in the first weeks of this second captivity is well rendered in a response she gave on February 27. This was a Tuesday, and Jeanne had been violently sick on Sunday after eating fish (a carp) that had been sent to her from Bishop Cauchon's

[36]Q, 3:204.
[37]Q, 5:382.

kitchen.[38] Doctors had been dispatched to the prison with the earl of Warwick's strict instruction to take good care of her because "the king did not at all want her to die a natural death. The king wanted to keep her; he had bought her at a high price; he did not want her to die, except in justice, burnt alive." The doctors examined her. They bled her in spite of the earl of Warwick's misgivings, and she was better. But one of them, Guillaume de la Chambre, the one who reported Warwick's warning, esteemed that her fever went up in an altercation she had with Jean d'Estivet, who was insulting her.[39] Because of her illness there was no session on Monday. On Tuesday the questioner, probably Jean Beaupère, for once in a friendly mood, asked how she had felt since Saturday: "You see that I have been as well as I can be."[40] In the circumstances she could not be expected to be very well, but she is as well as she can be. She remained as well as she could be during the whole trial until May 24, when she was led to the St.-Ouen cemetery.

During this time Jeanne's voices came to her every day, even several times a day, even in some of the sessions of the court. She did not always hear them well in the sessions or when the guards in her cell were noisy. But if she missed something they said they were soon back with her. They came by day and by night, on their own initiative and in answer to her prayer for help. They still spoke of King Charles. But their chief message was for her. They told her repeatedly to hold on, to answer *hardiment,* fearlessly, to take everything in good part; and they promised to lead her to paradise.

In the sessions of the court Jeanne was in a recurrent hassle with churchmen who, if at times they caught a glimpse of her spirituality of light, were too afraid of their political overlords to let such an insight influence their questions, insinuations, and

[38]The testimonies of two doctors mention the episode: Jean Tiphaine (Q, 3:48–9), Guillaume de la Chambre (51–2). Guillaume cites a doctor, Desjardins, who could be the same person as Tiphaine.

[39]Guillaume de la Chambre: Q, 3:49.

[40]2/27: T, 1:69: *Vous voyez que je me suis portée le mieux que j'ai pu* (Latin: *Vos bene videtis qualiter me habui. Ego me habui quantum melius potui*).

eventual conclusions. At the same time, however, Jeanne was in a quasi-permanent dialogue with the messengers of heaven. And therefore even at the worst moments of her imprisonment, deprived of sacraments, chained to a log, exposed night and day to the stare of English guards, fighting some attempts to rape her,[41] she still knew for certain that she was *la Pucelle,* the beloved daughter of God.

[41]There may have been several such attempts, all of them, it would seem, in Jeanne's last days. One of them, by her guards, was frustrated by the earl of Warwick, who responded to her cries for help (Q, 3:148). According to Ladvenu she was assaulted by *quidam magnus dominus anglicus* (Q, 3:168).

EIGHT

The Fire

The darkest point in the night that Jeanne underwent in prison descended on her suddenly in the octave of the feast of Pentecost, Wednesday, May 23 and Thursday, May 24. As far as Bishop Cauchon was concerned the trial was nearly over, the sentence arrived at: Jeanne was going to be solemnly condemned to life imprisonment. The ground for the sentence was her refusal to wear women's clothing. For the purpose of the trial her attitude in this peripheral matter was identified as a blatant rejection of the Church's authority. Jeanne's declarations of true faith and of love for the Church were irrelevant. The important point was that the court had declared her male garment to be indecent, immoral, a challenge to the laws of nature and the divine laws of the Church. By extension all that she said and did was tainted with rebellion and heresy. This is precisely the point of article 12:

> You have said that should the Church want you to act contrary to the command you say you have received from God you would not do it for anybody's sake; and that you know well that the points contained in this trial come from the command of God, and that it is impossible for you to do the opposite; and about them you do not want to abide by the judgment of the Church that is on earth or of any living person, but [you refer] to God alone. And moreover you say that you do not give these answers out of your own head but by the command of God, even though the article of faith *Unam sanctam* etc. has been explained to you many times, as also that all Christians are bound to place all their sayings and actions under the judgment of the Church Militant, especially in the matter of revelations and similar things.
>
> In regard to this the clerics say that you are schismatic, that you think wrongly of the unity and authority of the Church, that

you are apostate, and that until now you err pertinaciously in faith.[1]

Jeanne heard this last of the twelve articles of accusation on May 23. She could entertain no illusion as to the consequences. Pierre Maurice's charitable exhortation was clear. After reading and explaining this article he urged her to renounce everything she had said and done and to wait with humility for the tribunal's decision as to a suitable punishment for her innumerable crimes. Jeanne responded: "As to my actions and my words that I have said during the trial, I refer to them and I want to defend them. . . . The way I have always spoken and held in the trial I want to maintain."[2] The text adds: "Again she said that if she was sentenced and saw the fire lit and the faggots lit and the executioner ready to activate the fire and she was in the fire, she would say nothing else and she would defend what she has said in the trial, until death."

This was precisely what Bishop Cauchon hoped for. But since John of Lancaster expected more, he did not intend to sit still after finding her guilty of heresy, for such a charge could lead at most, according to the rules of the Roman Inquisition, to life imprisonment. This would be the first step. There would have to be a second step. In order to assuage his own conscience in the shady proceedings over which he presided, the bishop had to find her effectively relapsed, that is, falling again after professing to repent what the tribunal had determined to be her crimes. From the new crime of relapsing there could be no exit other than death. Thus the sentence that the duke of Bedford insisted on would be reached in keeping with the proper forms of ecclesiastical law: abandonment to the secular arm, which would then condemn the accused to death by fire. Having pushed *la Pucelle* into admitting her guilt and professing her acceptance of the Church's sentence, he now had to entrap her into rejecting this acceptance and rebelling against the Church. It was naturally assumed that she would at least implicitly identify the ecclesiastical court that condemned her with the Church militant. This maneuver was the purpose of the episode of May 24.

[1] T, 1:379–80.
[2] T, 1:383–84.

Thursday After Pentecost

The sentencing of Jeanne *la Pucelle* was scheduled for Thursday in the octave of the feast of Pentecost. Again the bishop's timing was deplorable, but he was obviously insensitive to the spiritual implications of the liturgical calendar. For the first time since the start of the trial the event would be open to the public. In the early morning Jeanne was therefore taken, for the first time also since her incarceration, outside the castle. According to secretary Manchon, Nicolas Loyseleur talked with her, at the door or in a passageway *(porta)*,[3] before she was led to the chariot; he urged her to save her life and submit to the court. He must also have brought a set of female clothes, since he is quoted as saying: "Jeanne, believe me, if you wish your life can be saved. Take this female dress and do all that will be asked of you; otherwise you are in danger of death. If you do what I tell you your life will be saved; you will gain more good and you will suffer no evil; you will be remitted to the Church."[4] At that moment Jeanne may still have believed that this man, an impostor, was truly from the Lorraine country and a genuine friend.

Jeanne was then accompanied by Jean Massieu, the usher who always led her to and from the tribunal, but this time they had a solid military escort. A chariot carried them through the narrow streets of the city to a cemetery that abutted the church of the abbey of St.-Ouen. A suitable platform had been erected for judges, lawyers, and a few distinguished visitors, and another, facing them, for her. Among the personalities who sat with the judges one could distinguish the cardinal of England, Henry Beaufort, bishop of Winchester. Massieu stood next to her. All around the scaffolding there were many soldiers and a great affluence of people.

The proceedings began with another charitable exhortation, pronounced by Guillaume Erard, professor of theology at the University of Paris. Erard had not attended the trial, but he had been present on May 9 when Jeanne was taken to the torture chamber. On May 10 he had voted against torture, for there

[3]Q, 3:146.
[4]Q, 3:145–46.

was already, he had declared, ample material for her condemnation.[5] In the open air and given the noise from the crowd the exact words of the speech may have been hard to catch. But Jeanne understood well a tirade when the orator denounced Charles VII as being "heretic and schismatic" by association with her and for believing in her. She interrupted him politely: "With all due respect, what you say is not true; I want you to know that there is no better Catholic among the Christians who are still alive."[6] This is confirmed in substance by other witnesses, notably Ysambard de la Pierre: "Preacher, you speak wrongly; do not speak of the person of my lord king Charles; he is a good Catholic and it is not in me that he has believed."[7] For Martin Ladvenu the preacher said: "O House of France, hitherto free of heretical monsters! Now you have prostituted yourself by believing this heretical and superstitious sorceress!" And Jeanne broke in: "Do not speak of my king; he is a good Christian."[8]

After Erard's peroration Jeanne spoke again: "I will answer. As regards submission to the Church, I have answered them [the judges] on this point. Let all the actions I have done and the words I have said be sent to Rome to our holy father the Pope, to whom—and first to God—I refer. As to the words and actions I have done, I have done them by God's command *[ex parte Dei]*. Again, as to what I have done and said, I blame no one, neither my king nor any other, and if there is some fault in them it comes from me and from no one else."[9] Being again asked if she will renounce what she has said and done she responded: "I refer to God and to our holy father the Pope."

[5]T, 1:351.

[6]Q, 2:335. The text of the exhortation is now lost. Erard would have said three times: "O kingdom formerly famed as Most Christian! O kings and princes formerly called Most Christian Kings! Behold through you, O Jeanne, your king who calls himself king of France has become heretical and schismatical by association with you and by believing your stories!"

[7]Q, 2:353. Erard is reported as saying, "France alone, formerly, was exempt of the monsters of heresy; but what an abominable monster has overpowered it today, when we see the one who calls himself the king of France rely on a schismatic, a heretic, and a witch for the recovery of his kingdom!"

[8]Q, 2:168.

[9]T, 1:387.

After Jeanne had spoken, three admonitions to recant were read, and as she did not comply the bishop of Beauvais began reading the prepared sentence. It was around nine o'clock. The sentence was a long and rambling speech that detailed the indictment and finally, in the last lines, announced that prison for life was the appropriate punishment that had been decided for the culprit.[10] In the meantime, Manchon recalled, Loyseleur found his way to the platform of the accused, ostensibly as an adviser. During the reading of the sentence Loyseleur "recommended to her that she do what he had said and take the female dress."[11]

The official record of the event states that Jeanne suddenly interrupted the bishop at an unspecified point before the end of the reading:

> She began to talk and she said that she wanted to abide by whatever the Church would order and whatever we judges would declare and decide, saying that she would entirely obey our ordinance. She said many times that once the churchmen said that the apparitions and revelations that she said she had could not be sustained or believed, she would not want to sustain them, but she completely referred to the holy mother Church and to us the judges.[12]

At that point a statement of abjuration was handed to her; it was read aloud by Massieu and she signed it.[13] Then the bishop read another prepared sentence, different from the one Jeanne had interrupted. It ended also with her condemnation:

> Because you have boldly sinned against God and the holy Church as previously stated we condemn you sententially and definitely to do salutary penance in prison for life with the bread of pain and water of sadness so that you may weep for your actions and you henceforth do not perform the actions you should weep for, always safeguarding our grace and moderation.[14]

---

[10]T, 1:413–15.
[11]Q, 3:146.
[12]T, 1:388–89.
[13]French and Latin text of this abjuration: T, 1:389–92.
[14]T, 1:393.

In the afternoon the vice-inquisitor led a small group of lawyers to Jeanne's cell in the tower to explain to her the meaning of what she had signed. They urged her "humbly to receive and obey the sentence and ordinance of the judges and churchmen, totally to forsake her previous errors and inventions, and in no way to return to them."[15] They specified that she must wear the female dress, since this was the court's order. Her reception "in the grace and mercy of holy mother Church" was contingent on it. Any return to her previous errors would force the Church to abandon her. Jeanne willingly accepted the dress and she let them shave off her hair as a sign of penance and submission.

Chaos in the Cemetery

So far the official account. But the redaction of this document was finalized several years after the facts by a team in which the Sorbonnard Thomas de Courcelles, a friend of Cauchon, had a major role. Comparison with the statements of a number of witnesses leads to the conclusion that the writers of the official version covered up what truly happened.

In reality the scene turned unruly after Erard's sermon and completely chaotic when the sentence was read. Erard held the text of an abjuration in his hand, and after his sermon he ordered Jeanne to sign it: "You will abjure and sign this document."[16] The text was passed on to Massieu, who was still standing next to Jeanne. Massieu read it to her. He later testified, "I know well that this document contained about eight lines,[17] no more; and I know absolutely that it was not the one that is mentioned in the acts, for what I read was different from what was included in the acts, and it was the text that Jeanne signed." In other words, there was a substitution of documents. The short one that

---

[15]T, 1:393–94. The lawyers included Nicolas Midi, Nicolas Loyseleur, Thomas de Courcelles, Ysambard de la Pierre, "and several others."

[16]Q, 3:156.

[17]This is confirmed by Nicolas Taquel, who said, "there were about six lines in big letters" (Q, 3:197).

Jeanne signed was replaced by the long one, which she had never seen and had not signed.

When Jeanne signed the short text she was under the illusion, presumably because she trusted Loyseleur, that she was going to be placed in a church prison. In fact she offered to sign it after being taken to a church prison: "Let this text be seen by the clerics and the Church in whose hands I must be placed; if they advise me to sign and do what I am asked to do I will be pleased to do it."[18] But Erard, Loyseleur, and probably others kept shouting that she must sign or she would be burned. Jeanne signed the text with a cross in a circle. Massieu reported growing confusion: "Then Jeanne said that she preferred to sign than to be burnt; at that moment there was a great turmoil among the people and stones were thrown." Secretary Manchon could not recall all the details: "During this time, Jeanne made it known that she was ready to obey the Church; then she was made to pronounce her abjuration by having the formula read to her. But I do not know if she repeated after the reader or if at the end of the reading she merely said that she agreed. She smiled. The executioner was present with a chariot, expecting that she be handed over to him for burning. . . . I do not remember that the content of this writ of abjuration was detailed or explained or even read to her before the moment of abjuration."[19]

There must have been a great deal of coming and going on Jeanne's platform, for according to Haimond de Macy, it was Laurent Calot, one of the secretaries of the king of England, who handed Jeanne the document she marked: "She said that she could not read or write. Nonetheless secretary Laurent Calot gave her the text and a pen for signing; as though in mockery Jeanne traced a kind of circle. Then Laurent Calot took her hand with the pen and made her trace a sign that I do not remember."[20] After signing Jeanne asked if she would now be "placed in the Church's hands" and where she would reside. But d'Estivet answered, "in the castle of Rouen."[21] And

---

[18]Q, 3:157.
[19]Q, 3:147.
[20]Q, 3:123.
[21]Massieu, Q, 3:157.

Cauchon ordered the guards: "Take her back where she came from."[22]

Whatever Jeanne said, whatever the reluctance of her signing and the elementary shape of her signature, Cauchon welcomed it as the total recantation he was seeking. That was the moment when an English priest who did not grasp what was going on got angry with him and called him a traitor; but the bishop retorted: "You lie; my profession obliges me to seek the salvation of her soul and her body."[23] The cardinal of England told the priest to be quiet.

Trinity Sunday and After

Let us return to the official minutes. Three days later, Trinity Sunday, May 27, around midday, Jeanne's guards reported to the earl of Warwick, who immediately informed Bishop Cauchon, that their prisoner had reverted to her male dress. In the afternoon several judges were called to the prison. Jeanne explained that her female dress was taken away by the guards, and although she argued with them for quite a while she had no choice but to put on the male clothes they brought her when she had to get up and go to the bathroom.[24]

On Monday, May 28, the bishop went to the prison with several of the judges. He saw that indeed Jeanne was in men's clothes. He asked why she was wearing them and who was responsible for it.[25]

[22]Q, 2:18.

[23]Pierre Miger: Q, 3:130.

[24]Massieu: Q, 3:157. This is the most likely reason for Jeanne's return to male clothes. Martin Ladvenu, however, heard "from Jeanne herself that a high personage of England *[magnus dominus anglicus]* came to see her in prison and attempted to assault *[opprimere]* her; and she said to him that this was the reason why she took up the male dress after the first sentencing" (Q, 3:168). Such a confidence could have been made shortly before Jeanne's death when Ladvenu heard her confession and gave her Communion. However, the reason for returning to male clothing does not tally with the one that is given by most witnesses. It is likely that Ladvenu placed an attempted rape at the wrong date.

[25]Jeanne's visitors of the day before must have reported that she had been entrapped into wearing male clothes.

By this time Jeanne had been able to think about the whole affair and to listen to her voices. "She answered that she had taken it up of her own will, under no pressure, and that she liked the male garment better than the female."[26] Under further questioning she protested that

> she never understood that she had pledged not to take it. . . . It was more licit to take it and to wear male clothing when she was among men than to wear women's clothes. . . . She had taken it because the promise made to her had not been kept, namely that she would go to mass and receive her Savior and she would not be in chains. . . . She would prefer to die than to be in chains, but if one is willing to let her go to mass and be kept without chains and in gracious prison with a female guard, then she will be good and do what the Church will want.

Jeanne went on: Yes, she had heard her voices since Thursday. They had blamed her in the name of God for "the great pity of the treason she had consented to by making abjuration and retractation to save her life, and that she was damning herself to save her life." Even before Thursday the voices had warned her of what she would do. On the scaffold they told her "to answer the preacher fearlessly, and she called him a false preacher because he said several things that she had not done. . . . If she said that God had not sent her she would damn herself; and truly God sent her. . . . Her voices had told her since Thursday that she had done a great misdeed by confessing that she had not acted well. . . . It was for fear of the fire that she said what she said." Indeed, her voices are those of St. Catherine and St. Marguerite. They come from God. In the trial she told the truth as best she could. On the scaffold she never intended to say that she had lyingly boasted that they were the saints Catherine and Marguerite; she had never denied or wished to deny her apparitions. In any case "she has never done anything against God or the faith, whatever she was ordered to retract, and she did not understand what was in the text of abjuration. . . . If the judges insist she is willing to take up the female dress, but no more."

On Tuesday, May 29, all judges and assessors were summoned to the chapel of the episcopal palace to determine the

[26]T, 1:396. The following citations are also from pages 396–99.

consequences of *la Pucelle's* spirited return to her errors. The unanimous conclusion was that she had relapsed. But the abbot of Fécamp spoiled this unanimity with the proviso that Jeanne be exhorted again: "She must be addressed with the word of God, and the text [of abjuration] must be read and explained to her." In other words, the abbot wanted Jeanne to be given another chance so that the court could be absolutely certain that she knew what she was doing when she relapsed.

Thirty-eight lawyers agreed that Jeanne should hear the text of her aburation once more. Nicolas de Venderez dissented: "She must be abandoned to secular justice."[27] Only one, the canon lawyer Denys Gastinel supported him. Another vaguely indicated that he would follow the doctors in theology. The bishop, however, thanked everybody, closed the meeting, and then ignored the position of the majority. Obviously Cauchon did not wish the long and detailed official abjuration to be read to Jeanne, because this was not the short text of six to eight lines she had signed in the growing turmoil of St.-Ouen cemetery.[28] One may then be certain that Cauchon himself, with the likely assistance of Venderez, was the perpetrator of a hoax, the substitution of the long text for the short one, to which the other lawyers were not privy. The hoax could have only one reason. The short text that Jeanne could sign in conscience would not have been sufficient to establish that she had abjured all her actions and that she had relapsed by returning to male clothes.

This, then, was what made Jeanne officially relapsed: She wore male dress when the bishop and his lawyers had determined that this was contrary to Christian and Catholic doctrine. The reasons for the male dress could be ignored. It was the doctrine that mattered, and it was the tribunal that determined the doctrine. Pierre Cauchon's promise of a beautiful trial ended up in a sinister *Grand Guignol* comedy. At any rate, the bishop carried out his plan. Following the consultation, without further ado he had a document drawn up: The accused was summoned to appear at the Old Market Square at eight o'clock the following

----

[27]All the opinions are recorded: T, 1:402–8.
[28]Thomas de Courcelles named Nicolas de Venderez as the author of the official abjuration: Q, 3:61.

morning, when she would be proclaimed "relapsed, excommunicate and heretic."[29]

The Burning

The happenings of the final day, May 30, 1431, at the Old Market Square were as weird as those of May 24 in the cemetery.

Two opposing logics were at work. On one side Jeanne reaffirmed all that the tribunal had condemned: she had really seen angels and saints, she had heard their voices, she had worn male dress with their agreement, she had been sent by them to the rescue of the kingdom of France. In this reaffirmation she underlined the inner logic of her calling, to which she had been faithful in all her wanderings of the last two years until she seemed to reject it in the confusion of the St. Ouen cemetery. On the other side there was the logic of the bishop of Beauvais. What was angelic in Jeanne's life was declared to be diabolical. Her light was darkness. She was an invoker of devils and demons, a liar about voices she pretended to hear, she reversed the order of nature and disobeyed the Church's teaching by dressing like a man, she found pleasure in the shedding of English blood. This was precisely the topic of a last formal exhortation, which was pronounced at the Old Market by Nicolas Midi, doctor in theology.

After the exhortation the bishop allowed two Dominicans, Martin Ladvenu and Ysambart de la Pierre, to assist the accused with charitable advice, and he pronounced the final sentence of a relapsed heretic: "We . . . declare that as a sick member you must be rejected from the unity of the Church in order not to infect other members, cut off from its body, and abandoned to the secular arm."[30] As was the custom he recommended mercy in carrying out the expected secular sentence of death by fire: "We beg the secular arm to moderate its sentence toward you before death and limb mutilation, and if signs of true repentance appear in you, that you receive the sacrament of penance."

A sermon by Nicolas Midi ended with a similar declaration of abandonment but robed this time in blatant hypocrisy:

[29]Q, 1:467–68.
[30]Q, 1:471–75.

"Jeanne, go in peace, the Church can no longer defend you and abandons you to the secular arm."[31] At these words, Massieu recalled, "Jeanne, kneeling, made her prayers to God with very great devotion and asked me for a cross; an English soldier who was there made one with a piece of wood, which she kissed and placed next to her heart with great devotion." While still on her platform Jeanne asked for a cross from the nearby church. "She got it and held on to it as she saluted the people present, then she went down the platform, still accompanied by Brother Martin; she went to the place of her execution, where she died most piously." Other witnesses reported that Jeanne cried, that she asked all the priests present to celebrate a Mass for her,[32] and above all, that she called the name of Jesus. It was also said that many of her enemies started crying too,[33] notably the cardinal of Luxembourg.[34]

But as things developed, several aspects of the proceedings were disconcerting. On the one hand the secular arm was in such a hurry to burn the victim that it ignored both the proper procedure and the recommendation of mercy. As the ecclesiastics withdrew from the scene Jeanne was immediately seized by the executioner and led to the pile of faggots. She was tied to a pole, and the faggots were immediately set on fire. All this was done in such a rush that no sentence of death was pronounced, as was required, by a secular court. From the standpoint of royal justice, therefore, the burning was itself illegal. Martin Ladvenu stayed with Jeanne when she was dragged to the pyre. She had time, as he reported, to see Pierre Cauchon and the canons of Rouen coming back to look. She was able to shout to him "that he was the cause of her death, that he had promised to place her in the hands of the Church, and that he had abandoned her to her deadly enemies."[35] When the fire started, she told Ladvenu to go. But the fire was so swift and the flames so high that the ex-

[31]Q, 3:159.
[32]Jean Lefèvre: Q, 3:177.
[33]Manchon: Q, 3:150; Guillaume Colles: 165; Mauger Leparmentier, 188.
[34]Jean Lefèvre: Q, 3:177; Andréa Marguerie: 185.
[35]Ladvenu: Q, 3:169.

ecutioner could not exercise the usual act of mercy toward those who were condemned to die by fire: he had no time before Jeanne was engulfed by flames and smoke to go up to her and strangle her.

On the other hand, the provision that Jeanne receive absolution if she showed signs of repentance was itself a piece of hypocrisy. For as Martin Ladvenu was to testify and several other witnesses to confirm, Bishop Cauchon had previously ordered Ladvenu to go to Jeanne in the early morning and to give her the sacrament of penance. In addition he had ordered him to bring her Communion.[36] This unusual disposition in favor of a person who has been declared a relapsed heretic was bound to intrigue the lawyers of the nullity inquiry. The list of topics on which witnesses were interrogated from 1452 to 1455 included the following item: "N. 23: That . . . although they had decided to give her the communion of the Body of Christ, . . . nonetheless, by complacency toward the English or by fear of them, they unjustly condemned her to the fire as a heretic.[37] In fact, Cauchon's decision to admit Jeanne to the sacraments on the last day of her life confirms under what logic he carried out her trial. As a pastor the bishop knew, or at least suspected, that Jeanne was totally innocent of all the crimes of which he was decided to find her formally guilty. It was only on the basis of such a conviction or suspicion that he could at least give her the benefit of the doubt and admit her to Communion. But as a canon lawyer he also considered that the sentence of guilty was justified by the letter of the law as this had been understood and carefully explained during the trial. The whole purpose of the proceedings had been precisely to establish the formal guilt of the accused, however perfectly innocent she could be and was. At the level of theology and conscience there was of course a price to pay for such an operation. The bishop had to ignore canonical equity in

[36]Q, 3:168. This is confirmed by others: Pierre Miget (Q, 2:363), Thomas de Courcelles (Q, 3:62), Jean Moreau (195), Nicolas Taquel (197).

[37]Q, 2:311–16. This is the list of twenty-seven topics composed by Guillaume Prévostin when he replaced Guillaume d'Estouteville. D'Estouteville's list had only twelve articles and was less detailed (Q, 2:292–95).

order to reach the conclusion that was demanded by the government of Henry VI. But canonical equity is by its very nature a matter of personal appreciation that remains open to question and contradiction. The letter of the law, on the contrary, can be so twisted as to provide safe protection for judges who pronounce a sentence they know to be unjust. Unscrupulous canon lawyers can easily do so.

Jeanne, however, was too pure-minded to suspect such a thing at the beginning of the trial. Because she loved the Church and believed that God and the Church were one, because she made no distinction in her heart between the Church triumphant and the Church militant, because she knew when she was visited by angels and saints that she herself belonged in the Church triumphant, she was unusually slow to recognize real sinfulness in the behavior of priests and bishops. She knew from the start, and she was hardly surprised by it, that the English wanted to make her die. Several times she warned the bishop to judge her justly or he would put himself in great danger. But only when the evidence of evil intent was overwhelming was she able to exclaim, "Bishop, I die through you."[38] The trigger of this belated recognition of grave defects in the men of the Church was Cauchon's order to keep her in the English prison after she agreed to wear the female dress. When she was forced to wear her male clothes again because the guards had taken the others away she finally realized that, bishop though he was, Pierre Cauchon did not care if she could no longer guard the virginity of her body. And although she was in distress and terror she neatly put the case to him: "If you had put me in the prisons of the ecclesiastical court and in the hands of competent and proper ecclesiastical guardians this would not have happened, and this is why I appeal to God against you." Jeanne in tears remained lucid as to what was important for the kingdom of God.

As Cauchon was pushing his canonical logic to its fiery end, it was really Jeanne's logic that asserted itself. To those who knew of her confession and Communion on the morning of May 30, Cauchon's duplicity underlined her simplicity. His double-

---

[38]Q, 2:3–4.

mindedness presupposed her single-mindedness and enhanced it. All witnesses testified that she died a good Christian. Some of them said that she called on her saints and on the archangel Michael. They all agreed that she called on Jesus as long as she was able. At the supreme moment when she found herself engulfed by the flames Jeanne held on to the cross while angels and saints gave way to the name of Jesus, the name that was on her standard and had led her to victory.

Conclusion

The spirituality of Jeanne *la Pucelle* cannot be neatly catalogued or classified. Jeanne herself was not trained in any of the spiritual disciplines known in her time. She belonged to no other school than that of the laity in a traditionally Catholic countryside. The means at her disposal to nurture her interior life were simply the sacraments, sermons, Latin prayers and hymns, processions, pilgrimages, churches, statues, and paintings that were available to all. Her way of holiness was general, not specific, public, not private, Catholic, not sectarian. It was focused on faith, not on devotional practices or forms of piety. As such it remains available to all believers in all ages of the Church.

There was nonetheless something that was quite specific and private in Jeanne *la Pucelle*'s way. And this was the special grace or graces that informed her discipleship of Christ. She received a grace of insight and of communication with God that was quite unique. Whatever psychological or other explanations may be suggested for the voices and lights that she heard and saw do not do away with the originality of her way. She was given spiritual perceptions that made her aware at the same time, in one and the same movement of attention, of heaven and of earth, of the world of angels and saints and of the world of humans, of the Church in heaven and of the Church on earth. The two levels of creation were one in her experience as they are one in the Creator's design and purpose. They coalesced in her awareness of the divine presence.

In this one motion of her soul Jeanne *la Pucelle* loved God and espoused the cause of justice on earth. The unity of heaven and earth she transferred with no hesitancy to human relations. Even if they are distinct virtues in the eyes of theologians, justice and charity function together. Loyal service of the king and fidelity to the human hierarchies of the kingdoms of earth and of the Church of God reflect the impact of the kingdom of paradise and of the Church in heaven on the terrestrial realities of everyday life. But such a conviction is so contrary to the politics of power that it runs into the reluctance or resistance of kings and their minions, as it also provokes the reactions of Church officials because it falls outside the scope of canon law. Her life offers a perfect example of the conjunction of contemplation and action, but this could not impress clergymen who found their own unity in political options.

It is not surprising that except for a few individuals most of Jeanne's contemporaries failed to see her where she was. They sought for her where she was not, in the imaginative world of the miraculous and the marvelous. Among the few who truly perceived at least some aspects of Jeanne's inner life I would count Charles VII himself in his better days and most probably the king's mother-in-law, Yolande d'Aragon, the theologian Jean Gerson, the bishop of Embrun, Jean Gélu,[1] and those leaders of the French who trusted her from the beginning of their acquaintance and did not withdraw their trust when the fortunes of war turned against her, namely, Bertrand de Poulengy and Jean de Nouillonpont, and also, higher in the hierarchy, Jean de Vignoles (La Hire), the duke Jean d'Alençon, Dunois, and the *connétable* de Richemont.[2]

Looking at the spiritual traditions of the fifteenth century one can find traces of Franciscanism and of Rhineland mysticism in Jeanne's life. Turning to what was still the future one can see

---

[1]Gélu's *Tractatus de puella aurelianensi* of May 1429 contains his considered judgment following Jeanne's interrogations in Poitiers; text in Q, 2:393–410.

[2]It is tempting to think that Charles's mistress, Agnès Sorel (ca.1422–1450), was among those who understood Jeanne, but Agnès was too young in Jeanne's time and was not yet at the court. It is possible, however, that she urged the king to find the truth about Jeanne's burning by his enemies. The reconquest of Rouen and the start of the investigation followed shortly after Agnès' unexpected death, when the king was certainly grieving. See Frank Hamel, *The Lady of Beauty* (London: Chapman & Hall, 1912).

anticipations of some insights of the *Imitation of Christ* and of the *devotio moderna* that was in the making in the Rhine valley. The Meuse river, by which Jeanne spent her childhood, flowed into the Rhine, and cultural influences not infrequently go up rivers and their tributaries.

It was the danger of war in the late nineteenth century that brought attention to Jeanne in her homeland, and it was after the miseries of the First World War that she was finally canonized. Jeanne, who went to battle with a flag and never fought with her sword, experienced peace in the middle of war. She is lifted up as an icon of peace in a time of turmoil and war. Humankind will need her example as long as it is pushed to war by its demons. Simone Weil has written: "Whoever uses the sword will die by the sword. And whoever does not use the sword (or lets it fall) will die on the cross."[3] Jeanne's cross took the form of imprisonment, harassment, and fire, but in the midst of it all she called on the name of Jesus, and God took her in his arms.

[3]Simone Weil, *Cahiers* (Paris: Librairie Plon, 1953) 2:135.

APPENDIX A

Jeanne's Womanhood

It has been said that Jeanne was not subject to the monthly period of women. This notion seems to derive from statements made at the nullity investigation, none of which affirms it. One possible source of the rumor is Jean Monnet's report that he had heard "that it was said at the time [of her examination for virginity] that her inferior parts had been damaged by horse-riding."[1] But the term *inferiora* is likely to refer to the shape of her legs, possibly somewhat misshapen by riding, or to scars on her thighs caused by riding for a long time in an armor rather than to her sexual organs. The other likely source of the rumor is Jean d'Aulon's testimony: "He also said that he had heard several women who several times had seen the said *Pucelle* nude and known her secrets say that she never had the secret disease of women and that nobody ever could know or notice anything of it from her garments or otherwise."[2] In other words, d'Aulon reported the sayings of gossiping women. The same Jean d'Aulon testified that Jeanne was examined in Poitiers under the supervision of the queen of Sicily (Yolande d'Aragon, the dauphin's mother-in-law): ". . . *la Pucelle* was seen, visited, and secretly viewed and examined in the secret parts of her body; but after they had looked at all that there was to see in that case, the said Lady said and reported to the king that she and her said ladies

[1] Q, 3:63.
[2] Q, 3:219.

found with certainty that she was a true and entire *pucelle*, in whom there was no trace of corruption or violence."[3]

This kind of examination was reiterated when Jeanne was in prison, this time under the supervision of the duchess of Bedford, assisted by two women that Massieu called "matrons or obstetricians," one of whom was named Anna Bavon. They reported "that she was a virgin and intact, and the duchess of Bedford had orders given to her guards not to do her any violence."[4] Boisguillaume concurred: "She was found to be a virgin," but he added that the duke of Bedford was watching the proceedings from a place of hiding.[5] This was also the conclusion of Guillaume de la Chambre, one of the doctors who looked after Jeanne when she got sick from eating fish: "He testified that he heard then that the same Jeanne had been examined to see if she was a virgin or not, and she was found to be; and he himself knows from what he could observe with the art of medicine that she was uncorrupted and a virgin, for he had seen her nearly nude when he examined her for a sickness."[6]

In these conditions the speculation of Abbé Villaret that Jeanne suffered from gynandria, a partial malformation of the female organs that makes sexual intercourse impossible, goes far beyond the evidence.[7] So does the notion, entertained by Marina Warner, that Jeanne suffered from anorexia.[8]

[3]Q, 2:209–10.
[4]Q, 3:155.
[5]Q, 3:162–63.
[6]Q, 3:50.
[7]Villaret, *Histoire de France en 30 volumes* (Paris, 1765), as summarized in Sermoise, *Les Missions*, 86, with note 64.
[8]Warner, *Joan of Arc*, 21–22.

APPENDIX B

Claude des Armoises

Before ending our study of Jeanne *la Pucelle*'s spiritual way it is appropriate to reflect on some bizarre happenings that followed her disappearance in flames and smoke at the Old Market Place of Rouen on May 30, 1431. These somewhat disturbing events are directly related to Jeanne's identity.

On May 20, 1436, barely six years after the drama of Rouen, a woman called Claude presented herself as being Jeanne *la Pucelle*, who, contrary to common belief, would not have died in Rouen! This unexpected revelation took place in the city of Metz in Lorraine at the parish church of St.-Thibaud. In the following month of August this Claude who claimed to be Jeanne married a nobleman of Lorraine, Robert des Armoises (d. before 1450), *seigneur* de Jaulny and Tichemont. The marriage took place at a residence of the duchess of Luxembourg in Arlon. Some time later this Claude/Jeanne des Armoises decided to pick up the career of Jeanne *la Pucelle* and to take up arms. She is said to have traveled to Rome and put her sword at the service of Eugene IV (pope, 1431–1447) to fight the antipope Felix V (1439–1449). She would have offered her services to Charles VII, who declined to entrust her with a mission. But the enterprising Gilles de Rais took her under his aegis, and for some two years she moved with his soldiery.[1] It is not clear whether Jeanne's brothers Jean and Pierre, who seemed to have been with her in Metz, spent time in her retinue.

---

[1] Jacques Heers, *Gilles de Rais,* 117–23. For this author and many others, Jeanne des Armoises was a vulgar impostor, *la fausse Jeanne d'Arc.*

174

According to some authors Jeanne des Armoises did no more than take part in "a few rides around Poitou, with no great lustre and no result: that was all."[2] For others she had a role in the conquest of the provinces of Languedoc and Guyenne; she was involved in a minor skirmish at La Rochelle and possibly near Le Mans; she entered Bayonne with the French army when the English garrison abandoned it. In any case she spent some time in Orléans, where she was received with honor in the summer of 1439, and on that occasion the city fathers suspended the celebration of Mass for *la Pucelle*. Although it has been said that Jeanne's ailing mother was herself staying in the city, from which she received a pension, there is no record of her presence in Orléans before August 1440. This was about the time when her son Pierre also settled in the Orléans area.

In 1441, after being seriously wounded, Jeanne des Armoises retired, and she thereafter lived with her husband in his house in Metz[3] and in the castle of Jaulny, where their joint portraits can still be seen above an ornamental chimney. She died in 1449 and was buried on the epistle side near the altar in the church of Pulligny, for the building of which Robert des Armoises and his wife may have made a donation. It seems that she had made frequent visits to her brother-in-law's château at Autrey to see her godchild, Louis des Armoises. Autrey is less than two kilometers from Pulligny. The two villages are some twenty kilometers south of Nancy. Unfortunately, the wall plaque that used to mark the location of the tomb was needlessly removed in 1890 when the beatification of Jeanne d'Arc was being considered.

The more common interpretation of these facts is that Claude (later, Jeanne) was a clever adventuress who exploited her uncanny resemblance to Jeanne Darc. Pierre and Jean du Lys would have joined her for a time in order to promote their career. If the king was taken in, it was only for a short time. She was summoned to appear before the Parliament of Paris in August 1444.[4] She may have been exiled from the kingdom, which

[2]Heer, *Gilles de Rais,* 122.

[3]The property in Metz faced the still-standing church of Ste Ségolène on what is now called, with some irony, *Place Jeanne d'Arc!*

[4]Jean Favier, *Dictionnaire de la France médiévale* (Paris: Fayard, 1993) 72. According to the Larousse dictionary Jeanne des Armoises

could not be much of a hardship, since her husband was a Lorrainer and his lands were not in France.

A number of revisionist authors, however, have accepted another version of the story.[5] In this version, Jeanne, also known as Claude, was in reality a half sister of Charles VII, an illegitimate daughter of the queen and the duke of Orléans, Louis II. There is some evidence that on or about November 10, 1407, the queen gave birth to twins, a boy named Philippe who did not live, and a girl named Jeanne. Knowing this, it is easy to imagine that this baby would have been unknown to King Charles VI and entrusted to foster parents, and that these were relatives of the Jeanne Darc who was known at the court as a maker of flower pieces. The child would then have been raised incognito at Domremy until somehow she was informed of her ancestry and some of her relatives in the know enjoined her to put her talents at the service of the dauphin. These she would have called her "voices."

The story raises two questions. There is the question of Jeanne's birth: in Paris as an illegitimate child of the queen, or in Domremy from Isabelle Romée, wife of Jacques Darc? And there is the question of her survival: Did Jeanne die in the fire as the tradition affirms and her canonization assumed, or did she escape from Rouen, go to exile in Lorraine, marry Robert des Armoises, have another short military career, and spend her last years in peace and with a degree of piety? The two problems should be carefully separated.

First, it is impossible to know for certain if Jeanne *la Pucelle* was truly what she seemed to be, the child of Jacques Darc, or a foster child of royal if illegitimate lineage. In the second hypothesis, her being received by the *dauphin* as one sent by heaven to help him recover the kingdom will be easier to under-

eluded the summons of the Parliament and the University of Paris, and Charles VII banished her from the kingdom in 1457. But in 1457 Jeanne des Armoises was dead and buried!

[5]Among other works, Pesme, *Jehanne* ; Sermoise, *Les Missions.* Pesme is extremely vague as to the identity and location of his sources. "De Sermoise" is a transformation of "des Armoises," and his presentation is largely based on family archives, genealogies, and traditions. But to what extent are these trustworthy? Tourists who visit the castle of Jaulny today are duly informed by the guide that Jeanne des Armoises was indeed Jeanne d'Arc.

stand if one is persuaded that God never intervenes in the affairs of this world through prophetic personalities who are given a divine mission. But one has then to posit a huge conspiracy in favor of Charles VII, which would have included false "voices" that revealed themselves to Jeanne under the cloak of secrecy at Domremy and that had access to her in the successive castles where she was a prisoner. This is remotely possible but most unlikely in view of the documentation of the trial and of the nullity inquiry. Moreover, there is no reliable evidence that some of her contemporaries believed, or professed to believe, that Jeanne was a royal princess.

Second, quite other is the suggestion that Jeanne escaped from Rouen. This hypothesis has to assume that the trial at Rouen was a farce put up for public consumption to reassure the English soldiery, the bishop of Beauvais, Pierre Cauchon, playing the two sides of the dynastic struggle with the connivance of the duke of Bedford. Cauchon pleased the English by finding Jeanne guilty of witchcraft, blasphemy, heresy, etc., but he favored Charles VII by making sure that Jeanne was taken away to safety through underground passages and eventually to a comfortable exile, while an anonymous witch was burned in her stead.

The hypothesis of Jeanne's survival runs counter to too many of Jeanne's sayings and to the responses that were recorded in the nullity inquiry to be acceptable. Charles VII was so convinced that Jeanne *la Pucelle* had indeed been burned in Rouen as a heretic that as soon as his soldiers entered the city in 1450 he ordered an investigation into the exact circumstances of the trial.[6] Pope Pius II (Aeneas Sylvius Piccolomini, 1405–1464, Bishop of Rome in 1458) did not believe that Jeanne escaped from Rouen and then reappeared a few years later. His "Commentary on the marvelous things that happened in his time" does contain a number of errors. Aeneas reports that Jeanne, daughter of a poor farmer, heard voices for the first time when she was watching a herd of pigs! He gives an account of the fall of Orléans, of the journey to Reims and the coronation, of the

---

[6] I need not speak of the additional fantasm that the conspiracy was led by the Third Order Franciscan, St. Colette and Yolande d'Aragon being its chief artisans!

unsuccessful assault on Paris. He mistakenly presents Jeanne's wound under the walls of Paris as the first she received and as a major surprise for her followers, who thought she was miraculously protected. He provides two different stories of her surrender to Jean de Luxembourg. He explicitly gives the fear and hatred of the English leaders as the most probable cause of her burning. He mentions that her ashes were thrown into the river Seine so that no cult of her could start around relics. And he concludes on the practical impossibility of reaching a final conclusion as to the origin of her deeds:

> Thus Jeanne died, the admirable and stupendous virgin *[virgo mirabilis et stupenda]* who restored the fallen and all but vanished kingdom of the Franks. . . . Whether this was a divine or a human work I would find it difficult to assert.[7]

The strange episode of Jeanne des Armoises would have no bearing on a study of Jeanne's spirituality if it did not draw attention again to the matter of self-identity. That Jeanne *la Pucelle* could be successfully impersonated by an enterprising woman to the point of letting many believe that the inquisitors who organized her official condemnation also engineered her escape is another facet of the fundamental anonymity of the girl from Domremy. Whether or not her two brothers were for a time in cahoots with an impostor or at least an impersonator, the claims of Jeanne des Armoises underline Jeanne *la Pucelle*'s basic spiritual feature. Her nothingness in her own eyes made it easier to overlook her in favor of a stranger with similar features who wished to imitate her and to prolong her action and who may have been, in a sense, inspired by her example.

The true Jeanne, straight and honest as she was, would have been shocked at the gall of Claude des Armoises pretend-

---

[7]Adrianus Van Heck, ed., *Pii II Commentarii rerum mirabilium que temporibus suis contingerint,* 2 vols. Città del Vaticano: Biblioteca Apostolica Vaticana, 1984, vol. 1, book 6, n. 10, p. 381–88; citation, p. 387. There exists an abbreviated translation of this work: Florence A. Gragg, trans., *Memoirs of a Renascence Pope: The Commentaries of Pius II. An Abridgment* (New York: G. P. Putnam & sons, 1959); on Jeanne d'Arc: pp. 201–9.

ing to take her place and to be her. She presumably would have appreciated the woman's gallantry on horseback and her courage if she really took part in some battles. She might have perceived the humor of the situation. Those who hold themselves to be no one leave room for others to take their name and their place and to bring them a renown that they have never sought. The inner void of Jeanne *la Pucelle* was, in her life, filled with God. But could it really matter to her if, after she died, it would seem to be filled with the person of Claude des Armoises?

In all of this, however, I see no ultimate reason to demean Jeanne des Armoises herself. It may be tempting to impersonate another if one has the capacity for it and the likelihood of a certain success. The serene features of Claude des Armoises and her husband, as they can still be seen above a fireplace in the castle of Jaulny, invite respect. So does their now unmarked resting place in the parish church of Pulligny.

APPENDIX C

The King's Pardon

If, as I think, Jeanne's spiritual simplicity was implicitly recognized by the bishop of Beauvais, this did not dim his devotion to the English cause on the Continent. But his hopes for a high ecclesiastical preferment as a reward for what he had done with Jeanne did not materialize. Although his name was duly put forward by John of Lancaster to succeed the late archbishop of Rouen, Cauchon obtained no more than a move from Beauvais to Lisieux. This was not a promotion. There he lived in wealth and comfort with his conscience until he died suddenly in 1442.[1]

Several of the judges and assessors of the trial, notably Thomas de Courcelles, did pursue a distinguished ecclesiastical career. Courcelles did not hesitate to change sides when necessary. At the Council of Basle he favored the conciliarist party, like most of the theologians from the Sorbonne. He even espoused the cause of Felix V (1439–1449), who made him one of his cardinals. Yet he later rallied behind Pope Nicholas V. Likewise he had no problem supporting Charles VII when the cause of Henry VI was irremediably lost by the reconquest of Normandy. He even pronounced the panegyric in praise of the king when Charles VII died in 1461. Yet if he had talent for maneuvering, Courcelles was hardly a great soul. He lied in some of the statements he made during the nullity investigation. In this, of course, he was not entirely alone, and most of the surviving judges or assessors were affected by serious memory lapses.

[1] According to Guillaume Colles, Cauchon's death occurred while he was being shaved by his barber, and Nicolas Midi soon died of leprosy (Q, 3:165).

In the recovery of the territories that the English party was forced to abandon one after the other, Charles VII stood by a principle of no revenge that was perfectly in the spirit of Jeanne's fighting. As his armies entered Normandy he signed letters of abolition that amounted to a general amnesty for actions taken against him and his cause on behalf of Henry VI and the English cause. Jeanne had affirmed in Rouen: "My king is a good Christian." A Christian king forgives. The principle even applied to those who had harassed and condemned Jeanne as well as to those who had profited from their collaboration with the English. No action was taken against any of her former detractors and adversaries, not excluding the only one, Jean Beaupère, who maintained in the nullity investigation that nothing was supernatural in her actions and that she was not innocent: "As to the innocence of Jeanne, she was most subtle with the subtlety of a woman, as it seemed to him."[2]

The episcopal successor of Cauchon, Guillaume de Hellande, bishop of Beauvais, was not cited to appear at the nullity investigation on his disclaimer that he wished in no way to defend his predecessor's actions and memory.[3] Cauchon's nieces and nephews, heirs to his wealth, were left in quiet possession as they invoked "the compositions and abolitions generously, mercifully, and benignly granted by our Lord the King in the recovery of our country of Normandy."[4] Yet the letter that was sent in their name by his grandnephew Jacques de Rivel admitted:

> According to what I heard and understood later (for at the time of the trial and sentence I was four or five years old, some of my brothers being younger, and some yet to be born), Jeanne was tried in a matter of faith through the jealousy and suggestion of the enemies of our Lord the King, because she was of his obedience and she caused them the greatest harm in the wars, and they wanted in this way to support their own party and quarrel, and if she had been of the party of the said enemies she would never have been tried in a matter of faith.[5]

[2] Royal inquiry of 1450: Q, 2:21.
[3] Q, 2:134.
[4] Q, 2:196.
[5] Q, 2:195–96.

Charles VII's forgiveness stands in sharp contrast with the duke of Bedford's ruthlessness: anyone who expressed support for *la Pucelle* was in danger of death. There had been a precedent for Jeanne's visions in those of Marie d'Avignon, who had prophesied to Charles VI that the kingdom would suffer many calamities and would be saved by a woman.[6] There was a sequel, and not only in the very suspect allegations of Catherine de la Rochelle or the military ambitions of Claude des Armoises. In Paris on September 3, 1430, a certain Pieronne, a woman from Brittany, was sentenced to die by fire because she maintained on the basis of her visions that Jeanne *la Pucelle* was a good person.[7] After Jeanne was captured a visionary shepherd, Guillaume de Mende, often called *le berger du Gévaudan,* or *le petit berger,* who was described by the "burgher of Paris" as having the stigmata, claimed to be divinely chosen to pursue her task.[8] He even had the endorsement of Jeanne's false friend, the archbishop of Reims Regnault de Chartres. The shepherd, however, was captured by the English outside Louviers around August 12, 1431 (in which episode Jeanne's friend Poton de Xaintrailles was also taken). The Burgundian chronicler Lefèvre de St.-Remy reports that he was exhibited in Paris on the occasion of Henry VI's coronation and then thrown into the river Seine.[9]

If John of Lancaster considered himself a Christian he was also a more modern man than his opponent Charles VII, who gave the example of Christian kingship in forgiving his enemies. The modern democracies rightly feel that justice should prevail, and to this end they have pursued the war crimes of the vanquished. Charles VII, however, knew that charity and forgiveness overrule human justice and that ignoring them is itself a breach

[6]There were several forms of the prophecy, which was attributed to several seers. Though she may not have known about Marie d'Avignon, Jeanne alluded to it, as did several witnesses in the nullity inquiry: Durand Laxard (Q, 2:444); Catherine le Royer (Q, 2:447); Jean Barbin (Q, 3:83–84).

[7]Tutey, *Journal,* "Jeanne d'Arc," 236–70 (n. 503–78); "Jeanne des Armoises," 354–55 (n. 789–91): same references in Geneva: Slatkine Reprints, 1975.

[8]Tutey, *Journal,* 272 (n. 581); Q, 5:168–69.

[9]Tutey, *Journal,* 272, note 2.

of the justice of the kingdom of God. In forgiving the crimes of his enemies he behaved as the lord of what Jeanne had called "the holy kingdom of France" in the letter by which she invited the duke of Burgundy to attend the coronation in Reims.[10] Jeanne and her king still have a political lesson to teach that the modern age has failed to learn.

[10]Q, 5:126–27.

APPENDIX D

Posthumous Information?

The document entitled *Posthumous Information* (June 7, 1431)[1] alleges that on May 30 around seven o'clock in the morning, Pierre Cauchon, Thomas de Courcelles, Pierre Maurice, Nicolas de Venderès, Jean Le Camus, Nicolas Loyseleur, and the Dominicans Jean Toutmouillé and Martin Ladvenu visited Jeanne for a last-minute interrogation. She would then have admitted that the voices had lied to her and that she had also lied to the judges.

This information is not corroborated. Not one witness mentions the incident or the document, not even Courcelles, Maurice, Toutmouillé, or Ladvenu. The only reference is secretary Manchon's statement that he refused to sign it. In addition, it is most likely that Cauchon would have brought in the vice-inquisitor Jean Lemaire if he truly expected a final recantation. Moreover, Jeanne's alleged confessions are totally out of character (She herself was the angel of the crown!) and even absurd (She often saw angels as dots of light!).

There is every reason to regard this report as a fake, the falsification being concocted under Cauchon's orders, in part to justify his admission of Jeanne to Communion on the basis of a last-minute repentance, in part to suggest a natural explanation for her visions: she would have suffered from severe anemia, that was the cause of her visions and voices!

[1]Q, 1:447–85.

APPENDIX E

Chronology
of Relevant Information

The Dates of Jeanne d'Arc

1407/8 or 1411/12
Jeanne is born in Domremy.

1420
Treaty of Troyes

1420 or 1424/25
Jeanne hears her voices for the first time.

1424
Domremy is burned by Burgundian/English soldiers while the people take refuge in Neufchâteau.

1428
October 12: The siege of Orléans begins.
Late fall: Jeanne goes to Vaucouleurs, meets with Robert de Baudricourt, asks to be sent to Chinon.

1429
Early February: Jeanne visits the duke of Lorraine in Nancy.
February 23: Jeanne starts for Chinon with an escort.
March 8: Jeanne meets the dauphin in Chinon.
March/April: Jeanne is interrogated by churchmen in Poitiers.
April 5: Jeanne is equipped as a soldier in Tours.
April 29: Jeanne enters the besieged city of Orléans.

May 7: Jeanne is wounded in the assault on Fort Les Tourelles.

May 8: The English give up the siege of Orléans.

June 18: The English army is routed at Patay.

July 17: The dauphin is crowned in the cathedral of Reims.

September 7–8: Attack on Paris; Jeanne is wounded.

September 21: The king dissolves the bulk of his army.

1430

April: Jeanne leaves the court at Sully-sur-Loire.

May 23: Jeanne is captured by Burgundians under the walls of Compiègne.

May 27: Jeanne is a prisoner of Jean de Luxembourg at his castle of Beaulieu-les-Fontaines.

July 11: Jeanne is in Jean de Luxembourg's castle of Beaurevoir.

Early November: Jeanne tries to escape by leaping from a window.

Late November: Jeanne is sold by Jean de Luxembourg to the duke of Bedford.

December: Jeanne is transferred to the castle in Rouen and kept in strict confinement.

1431

January 9: The trial of Jeanne begins.

May 24: Jeanne is sentenced to life in prison.

May 30: Jeanne is handed over to the secular arm and burned on the Place du Vieux Marché.

1435

September 20: The Peace of Arras is signed between Charles VII and the duke of Burgundy.

1436

April 13: The French army enters Paris.

1449

November 10: Charles VII enters Rouen.

1450

February 13: Charles VII orders an investigation of the trial.

1452
> April: The inquisitor Jean Bréhal begins an investigation of the trial.

1455
> June 11: Pope Calixtus III orders an investigation of the trial.

1456
> July 7: The trial and condemnation of Jeanne are solemnly declared null and void by the archbishop of Rouen.

1909
> April 18: Jeanne is beatified by Pope Pius X.

1920
> May 16: Jeanne is canonized by Pope Benedict XV.

The March of the Trial

The usual course of an Inquisition trial went through two phases. A first phase, *processus preparatorius vel officio,* was in the form of an investigation of whatever the accused was suspected of; it ended either with the release of the accused or with the drawing up of formal articles of accusation. A second phase, *processus ordinarius,* was a confrontation of the accused with the articles of accusation. It ended with sentencing according to the evidence. To face the charges and respond to them the accused stood normally alone, without the help of a lawyer for the defense. An exception to this rule was that a minor accused in a matter of faith must have such a lawyer. Except for capacity to marry, the age of majority was twenty-five years: Jeanne *la Pucelle* was younger.

In the case of Jeanne there were actually three phases, or, if one prefers, there were two trials. The two standard phases of the first trial ended when she was sentenced to prison for life. But she was briefly tried for "relapsing" into heresy when she was seen wearing male clothes after agreeing to give them up. The inevitable penalty for relapsing was abandonment to the secular arm, followed by being sentenced by a secular judge to death by burning. Jeanne, however, was burned forthwith, without a formal sentencing by a secular judge.

Preparatory Phase (called, "Trial of Office")

1st session, February 21, 1431
    altercation on swearing to tell the truth. This recurs practically
        at the start of all the sessions. On the one hand, Jeanne
        does not want to tell the judges what they should not
        know. On the other, she sees no point in taking the same
        oath more than once.
    details on Jeanne's name and origin
    on her religious knowledge
    on saying the Lord's Prayer
    she refuses to promise not to escape

2nd session, February 22
    account of her life

3rd session, February 24
    altercation about taking an oath again
    questions on her voices
    about the Fairies' Tree

4th session, February 27
    about the voices
    identification of the two saints
    identification of the archangel Michael
    about her male dress
    about the light
    about the sword
    about her standard
    about the battles of Orléans and Jargeau

5th session, March 1
    who is the true pope?
    about her letter to the king of England
    her prophecy of a great victory
    how does she see her voices?
    her rings, the Tree, a mandrake
    about St. Michael
    about the sign of the crown

6th session, March 3
 about the shape of angels and saints
 about her male dress
 about her standards, rings, people who kissed her hands
 about Catherine de la Rochelle
 about her leap from a tower of Beaurevoir

Complementary Interrogations

7th session, March 10
 on her capture
 on her standard
 on her horses and wealth
 on Catherine de la Rochelle
 on the sign to the king

8th session, March 12
 on the angel who gave the sign to the king
 on her promise of virginity
 on obedience to parents
 on her father's dreams
 on freeing the duke of Orléans

9th session, March 13
 on the sign to the king

10th session, March 14
 on her leap at Beaurevoir
 on her voices
 on her assurance of salvation
 on the execution of Franquet
 on her being in mortal sin

11th session, March 15
 on her attempt to escape from Beaulieu
 promise to let her attend Mass if she changes to female dress
 on the cult of saints
 on her guilt

12th session, March 17
 on St. Michael
 prediction of a French victory

on the Church, triumphant and militant
on her dress
on whether God hates the English
on her offering to St. Denys
on her standard
on obedience to the pope
on her rings

Ordinary Phase (called "Ordinary Trial")

March 2: Judges and assessors agree on seventy articles of accusation.

March 27–28: Jeanne is read the seventy articles of accusation. She responds to most of them.

March 31: Jeanne is asked if she will submit to the Church militant.

April 2: Judges and assessors decide to reduce the accusation to twelve articles.

April 5: Judges and assessors agree on twelve articles of accusation. In the next few weeks they hand in their written comments on the articles.

April 18: Jeanne, sick, is visited in prison by Cauchon and others. She asks for confession, Communion, and burial in holy ground. Questions about her revelations and the saints. Offer of counsel. Various exhortations.

May 2: Exhortation in six points by Jean de Châtillon. Questions on the Church militant, on revelations, on knowing the future.

May 9: In the torture chamber.

May 12: Torture is rejected: eleven assessors are against it, three for it.

May 19: The opinion of the University of Paris on the twelve articles of accusation is examined. The lawyers give their opinion as to Jeanne's guilt.

May 23: The twelve articles of accusation are read to Jeanne by Pierre Maurice, who delivers his exhortation, *Amica carissima*. Questions as to whether she will submit to the Church militant.

May 24: In the St. Ouen cemetery Jeanne is sentenced to life imprisonment. Jeanne's alleged abjuration: she agrees to wear female vestments.

Trial for "Relapsing"

May 28: Jeanne is accused of relapsing into witchcraft and heresy because she has changed back to male clothes. She retracts all abjuration she may have made.

May 29: Judges and assessors unanimously find her relapsed and agree that she must be abandoned to the secular arm.

May 30: On the Market Place of Rouen Jeanne is sentenced to be abandoned to the secular arm. She is immediately taken by soldiers and burned.

Bibliography

Texts

Doncoeur, Paul. *La Minute française des interrogatoires de Jeanne la Pucelle.* Melun: Editions d'Argences, 1952.

Duparc, Pierre. *Procès en nullité de la condemnation de Jeanne d'Arc.* 3 vols. Paris: Klincksieck, 1977, 1979, 1983.

Oursel, Raymond. *Les Procès de Jeanne d'Arc.* Paris: Denoël, 1959.

Quicherat, Jules. *Procès de condamnation et de réhabilitation de Jeanne d'Arc, suivis de documents historiques.* 5 vols. Paris: Jules Renouard, 1841–49.

Tisset, Pierre. *Procès de condamnation de Jeanne d'Arc.* 3 vols. Paris: Klincksieck, 1960, 1970, 1971.

Tuetey, Alexandre, ed. *Journal d'un bourgeois de Paris (1405–1449).* Geneva: Slatkine reprints, 1975.

Selected Studies

Barnay, Sylvie. *Les Apparitions de la Vierge.* Paris: Le Cerf, 1992.

Bastaire, Jean. *Pour Jeanne d'Arc.* Paris: Le Cerf, 1979.

Beevers, John. *St. Joan of Arc.* Rockford, Ill.: Tan Books, 1974.

Bordonove, Georges. *Jeanne d'Arc et la guerre de 100 ans.* Paris: Pygmalion, 1994.

Burne, Alfred. *The Agincourt War: A Military History of the Latter Part of the Hundred Years' War from 1369 to 1453.* Fair Lawn, N.J.: Essential Books, 1956.

Bynum, Caroline Walker. *Holy Feast and Holy Fast: The Religious Significance of Food to Medieval Women.* Berkeley: University of California Press, 1988.

192

Champion, Pierre. *Vie de Guillaume de Flavy, capitaine de Compiègne. Contribution à l'histoire de Jeanne d'Arc et à l'étude de la vie militaire et privée au XVe siècle.* Paris: Honoré Champion, 1906.

_____. *Procès de condamnation de Jeanne d'Arc.* 2 vols. Paris: 1920–21.

Dominique, Pierre. *L'inquisition.* Paris: Libraire Académique Perrin, n.d.

Endore, Guy, *The Sword of God.* New York: Farrar and Reinhart, 1931.

Gies, Frances. *Joan of Arc: The Legend and the Reality.* New York: Harper & Row, 1981.

Heers, Jacques. *Gilles de Rais.* Paris: Perrin, 1994.

Levron, Jacques. *Le Bon Roi René.* Paris: Arthaud, 1972.

Lightbody, Charles Wayland. *The Judgements of Joan.* Cambridge, Mass.: Harvard University Press, 1961.

Lucie-Smith, Edward. *Joan of Arc.* New York: W. W. Norton, 1976.

Marot, Pierre. *Jeanne la Bonne Lorraine à Domremy.* Colmar: Editions S.A.E.P., 1980.

McLeod, Enid. *Charles of Orléans, Prince and Poet.* New York: The Viking Press, 1969.

Moinot, Pierre. *Jeanne d'Arc. Le pouvoir et l'innocence.* Paris: Flammarion, 1988.

Paine, Albert Bigelow. *Joan of Arc, Maid of France.* 2 vols. New York: Macmillan, 1925.

Parisse, Michel, ed. *Histoire de la Lorraine.* Paris: Privat, 1978.

Pernoud, Régine. *Vie et mort de Jeanne d'Arc.* Paris: Hachette, 1972.

_____. *La Femme au temps des cathédrales.* Paris: Editions Stock, 1980.

_____. *La Spiritualité de Jeanne d'Arc.* Paris: Mame, 1992.

Pesme, Gérard. *Jehanne n'a pas été brûlée.* Angoulême: Editions Balzac, 1960.

Petit de Julleville, Louis. *La Bienheureuse Jeanne d'Arc.* Paris: Gabalda, 1909.

Petroff, Elizabeth Alvilda. *Body and Soul: Essays on Medieval Women and Mysticism.* New York: Oxford University Press, 1994.

Rankion, Daniel, and Claire Quintal. *The First Biography of Joan of Arc*. Pittsburgh: University of Pittsburgh Press, 1964.

Sackville-West, V. *Saint Joan of Arc*. New York: The Literary Guild, 1936.

Scott, W. S. *Jeanne d'Arc*. London: Harrap & Co., 1974.

Sermoise, Pierre de. *Les Missions secrètes de Jehanne la Pucelle*. Paris: Robert Laffont, 1970.

Stolpe, Sven. *The Maid of Orleans*. New York: Pantheon Books, 1956.

Warner, Marina. *Joan of Arc: The Image of Female Heroism*. New York: Knopf, 1981.

Wheeler, Bonnie, and Charles T. Wood, eds. *Fresh Verdicts on Joan of Arc*. New York: Garland Publishers, 1996.

Index